SACRAMENTS

of

HEALING

SACRAMENTS

of

HEALING

METROPOLITAN KALLISTOS WARE

Foreword by Archpriest Andrew Louth
Edited by Rev. Ignatius Green

ST VLADIMIR'S SEMINARY PRESS

YONKERS, NY 10707

2023

Publisher's Cataloging-in-Publication
(Provided by Cassidy Cataloguing Services, Inc.).

Names: Kallistos, Bishop of Diokleia, 1934-2022, author. | Louth, Andrew, writer of foreword. | Green, Ignatius, editor.
Title: Sacraments of healing / Metropolitan Kallistos Ware ; foreword by Archpriest Andrew Louth ; edited by Rev. Ignatius Green.
Description: Yonkers, NY : St Vladimir's Seminary Press, [2023] | Includes bibliographical references.
Identifiers: ISBN: 978-0-88141-741-8 (paperback) | 978-0-88141-742-5 (Kindle) | LCCN: 2023935988
Subjects: LCSH: Healing--Religious aspects--Orthodox Eastern Church. | Spiritual healing--Orthodox Eastern Church. | Sacraments--Orthodox Eastern Church. | Spiritual formation--Orthodox Eastern Church. | Christian life--Orthodox Eastern authors. | Death--Religious aspects-- Orthodox Eastern Church. | Orthodox Eastern Church--Doctrines. | BISAC: RELIGION / Christian Rituals & Practice / Sacraments. | RELIGION / Christian Theology / Anthropology. | RELIGION / Christian Living / Death, Grief, Bereavement. | RELIGION / Christian Living / Spiritual Growth.
Classification: LCC: BX378.H4 K35 2023 | DDC: 234/.16--dc23

Copyright © 2023
St Vladimir's Seminary Press
575 Scarsdale Rd, Yonkers, NY 10707
1–800–204–2665
www.svspress.com

ISBN 978-0-88141-741-8 (paperback)
ISBN 978-0-88141-742-5 (Kindle)

PRINTED IN CANADA

The publication of this book was made possible by a generous gift from Gregory and Jeanette Swenson. Other donors include Mr Brian Mustapich, Rev. Elias Dorham, and Ms Pamela Cousoulis.

Contents

Foreword   ix

Chapter 1   "Glorify God with Your Body"   1

Chapter 2   The Passions: Enemy or Friend?   17

Chapter 3   Approaching Christ the Physician:
            The True Meaning of Confession
            and Anointing   33

Chapter 4   "In Peace Let Us Pray to the Lord":
            Peace and Healing in the Divine Liturgy   57

Chapter 5   "Let Us Go Forth in Peace":
            Healing in the Parish, in the Local Church,
            and in the World   73

Chapter 6   "A Peaceful Ending to Our Life":
            Bodily Death as an Experience of Healing   91

Abbreviations   111

Endnotes   113

Foreword

Metropolitan Kallistos was a supreme master of communication. Indeed, it would be fair to say that, as a thinker and theologian, he valued communicating to other people far more than intervening in theological debate or creating a fresh and appealing approach to Orthodox theology (he had many research students but left no "theological school"). He could have made a name for himself as a leading figure in the Orthodox theological world—or indeed in the wider Christian world—but that either did not interest him, or he simply valued communicating: he could well have made his own a phrase from St Thomas Aquinas' *Summa Theologiae*, which has become the motto of the Order of Preachers—the Dominican Order—*contemplata aliis tradere*, "to pass on to others things contemplated."[1]

---

[1] *Summa Theologiae* IIa IIae, q. 188, a. 6, resp.; cf. IIIa, q. 40, a. 1, ad 2.

These talks are a supreme example of Met. Kallistos' passing on to others what he has contemplated: a supreme example, perhaps because they were delivered to a group to whom he felt close—at a retreat for members of the Orthodox Peace Fellowship, founded by Jim Forest in 1986, with which Bishop Kallistos had been associated from its earliest days (the first hierarch to join the advisory board). The retreat was held at Vézelay in central France toward the end of Bright Week in 1999. In another way this book could be regarded as a supplement to his book, *The Orthodox Way*, published in 1979, from catechetical talks given by the Metropolitan in his parish in Oxford. He had intended a companion volume, dealing with the doctrines of the Church and the sacraments, but never found the time to bring it together. Much of the present book, *Sacraments of Healing*, would have found its way into such a book; all that would have been needed would have been for the chapters to be supplemented by patristic florilegia ("patristic" understood in a broad sense).

When presenting Orthodoxy—whether in a book or series of talks, or even in a single lecture—Met. Kallistos was always conscious of the wider ramifications of Orthodoxy. And so in this case. Apart from the talks being tailored to the concerns of members of the Orthodox Peace Fellowship—as we shall see in a moment—the Metropolitan sets out the foundations of any Orthodox consideration of the sacraments, and this he does in the first two lectures, on subjects that might seem unusual, given the title of the book. They concern the body and its place in an Orthodox Christian way of life, and indeed in an Orthodox understanding of the world in which we live—that is the subject of the first lecture, which is continued in the second lecture on what we call the "passions," for want of a better word. For the bodily and material is placed in the foreground in any consideration of the sacraments. As David Jones, the Anglo-Welsh poet, once remarked,

> No wonder then that Theology regards the body as a unique good. Without body: no sacrament, Angels only: no sacrament. Beasts only: no sacrament. Man: sacrament at every turn and all levels of the "profane" and "sacred," in the trivial and in the profound, no escape from sacrament.[2]

[2] David Jones, "Art and Sacrament," in David Jones, *Epoch and Artist* (New York: Chilmark Press, 1959), 166–67.

Any form of Christianity worthy of the name is bound to have a positive view of the bodily and material, for this is part of God's creation, which is good. Nevertheless, there are forms of Christianity that seem reluctant to recognize this, so we need to be clear about it. The quotation from David Jones also sees the human as central to sacramentality: it is humans, consisting of body and soul, who make and recognize sacraments. The centrality of the human—anthropocentricity—is part of the Christian notion of a sacramental cosmos, which confers on humans a far-reaching responsibility for the world in which they live. All this Met. Kallistos draws out, before turning to the sacraments themselves. But there is more: human beings, as we know them, are disordered as a result of what we call the Fall, and this disorder manifests itself in disjunction between the body and the soul, and indeed in both considered on their own. Awareness of this can lead to a tendency to denigrate the body, a Manichaean tendency not unknown in Orthodox ascetic circles. Met. Kallistos, patiently and gently, introduces considerations that weigh against any such tendency—considerations that begin from the human capacity for wonder.

"Sacraments of healing"—sacraments that restore the wholeness and balance of the human person. All sacraments play their part in this restoration, but in these talks the Metropolitan is selective. A chapter on Confession, as well as sacred Anointing, often called the Sacrament of Healing (for one is anointed with oil "for healing of soul and body") explores our encounter with Christ the Physician, the Healer. There follow two chapters on the Divine Liturgy—that is, the service itself, and what has come to be called the "liturgy after the Liturgy." The focus of these two chapters is the petitions for peace in the litanies, beginning with the first three petitions of the opening litany, called the "Litany of Peace" (or, in the Greek: *Eirenika*):

> In peace, let us pray to the Lord.

> For the peace from above and for the salvation of our souls, let us pray to the Lord.

> For the peace of the whole world, for the welfare of the holy churches of God, and for the union of all, let us pray to the Lord.

Met. Kallistos develops from these three petitions an understanding of peace that begins in the heart, which receives it "from above," and spreads to all human beings, the whole world (not just the human world, but the whole, all-embracing cosmos), and the union of the whole creation. He goes on to register the continued recourse to peace: the priest's greeting "Peace be unto all," repeated throughout the Liturgy; the giving of the kiss of peace (rarely, alas, now among the laity); through to the priest's dismissal, "Let us depart in peace." And, finally, death as a "peaceful ending to our life"—from a petition repeated twice in the course of the Liturgy. Met. Kallistos' discussion echoes his discussion of the passions—both death and passion refer to something that happens to us, but which also, in the case of our Lord, are described as "voluntary," deliberately accepted, not just endured—of both we can ask: "friend or foe?"

Metropolitan, Bishop, Father Kallistos—for those who knew him he remained, and remains, "Father Kallistos"—is instantly recognizable in these talks: there is the use of stories, often relating to himself (though never drawing attention to himself), a sense of lightness, even of humor, that lies beneath the seriousness of his subject matter. A further characteristic is his easy reference to quotations: sayings, remarks by the Fathers (a term he used, as did one of his mentors, Fr Georges Florovsky, in a broader sense than is common—not just the ancient Fathers, but our fathers in the faith from the beginnings to the present day, sometimes indeed "fathers in faith," not just the Christian faith, and certainly embracing "mothers")—anyone who has seen his card index, running to what must be thousands of entries, can testify to the diligence with which he created this resource, more for teaching, than for research: and not only Fathers, but also poets. These talks are the fruit of enormous learning (though worn very lightly), but also of many years of pastoral experience, and furthermore a lifetime of prayer, both liturgical (Met. Kallistos was an inspiring liturgist, in the proper sense of that word—one who makes liturgy, rather than one who studies it) and private (though never paraded). Memories of his pastoral experience will fade (though a book like this bears eloquent witness to it), even the card index, though it will provide a resource for many years, will be less and less consulted, but the prayer of our dear Father Kallistos will endure—"now and ever and unto the ages of ages."

—Archpriest Andrew Louth

1

"Glorify God with Your Body"

Orthodox Peace Fellowship retreat in Vézelay, April 1999

In April 1999, at the end of Bright Week, Bishop Kallistos of Diokleia led a retreat for members of the Orthodox Peace Fellowship. Our host was the parish of Saint Étienne and Saint Germain in the village of Vézelay, France. This is the first of six lectures. Bishop Kallistos was Spalding Lecturer in Eastern Orthodox Studies at the University of Oxford and led the Greek parish in the same city. His books include The Orthodox Church *and* The Orthodox Way.

First let me apologize for arriving late. I missed my train at the Gare de Lyon, and then I got on the wrong train, one that wasn't going to stop at Laroche-Migennes but was going to Dijon. They stopped in Laroche-Migennes especially for me. That is the first time I have had that experience. I am thinking in very high terms of the French railway. I cannot imagine the British railways making an unscheduled stop.

Our theme is "Sacraments of Healing." Please think of the word *sacrament* and what it signifies. Saint Nicholas Cabasilas says, "It is the sacraments that constitute our life in Christ."[1] Let us root our thinking in the sacraments. Saint Nicholas Cabasilas also called the sacraments "windows into this dark world."[2]

Yes, it is a dark world. I am sure for all of us present that our celebration of Pascha has been overshadowed by the immense human tragedy in Kosovo.[3] I recall how the bombing commenced on the feast on the Annunciation, according to the new calendar. It continued throughout the Holy Week and Pascha and there is no sign of its ending. We think of all the refugees. How many people's lives have been utterly wrecked?

But though we live in a dark world, there are windows into it. Let us remember the Greek term for sacrament—*mystērion*, mystery. This has a whole range of associations that the Latin word *sacramentum* lacks. A mystery, in the true religious sense, is not simply an enigma, an unexplained problem. A mystery is something that is revealed for our understanding, yet never totally revealed because it reaches into the infinity of God. The mystery of all mysteries is the incarnation of Christ; therefore, all other sacraments of the Church are founded upon that.

The second word in my title that we shall need to keep in mind during these days is *healing*—Sacraments of Healing. Healing means wholeness. I am broken and fragmented. Healing means a recovery of unity. Let us each think that I cannot bring peace and unity to the world unless I am at peace and unity with myself. "Acquire the spirit of peace," says Saint Seraphim of Sarov, "and thousands around you will find salvation."[4] If I do not have the spirit of peace within myself, if I am inwardly divided, I shall spread that division around me to others. Great divisions in the world between nations and states spring from many divisions within the human heart of each one of us.

I want to start with the human person. How I am to understand my unity as a person? What models do I have when I think of the healing of my total self?

I would like to share with you a patristic model, a recurrent model in the Fathers that can be summed up in the words *microcosm* and *mediate*. Human beings are a complex unity. My personhood is a single whole, but a whole that embraces many aspects. As humans we stand at the center and crossroads of the creation. Saint John Chrysostom thinks of the human person as bridge and bond. In a Sufi phrase quoted by Pico della Mirandola, the human person is "the marriage song of the world."[5] Each of us then, is a little universe, a microcosm, each of us is *imago mundi*—an icon of the world. Each reflects within himself or herself the manifold diversity of the created order. This was a recurrent theme in various pagan authors and was taken over by the early Fathers.

"Understand," says Origen, "that you have within yourself on a small scale a second universe. Within you there is a sun, there is a moon, there are also stars."[6] This theme is developed in a celebrated passage by Saint Gregory Nazianzen, the Theologian. In his 38th Oration, he distinguishes the two main levels of the created order.[7] On one hand there is the spiritual or invisible order, on the other there is the material or physical order. Angels belong only to the first order. They are bodiless, spiritual beings. In Saint Gregory's view, animals belong to the second order—the material and physical. You, uniquely in God's creation, exist on both levels at once. *Anthrōpos*, man, the human person alone, has a twofold nature, both material and spiritual. Saint Gregory goes on to speak of ourselves as earthly yet heavenly, temporal yet immortal, visible yet intelligible, midway between majesty and lowliness, one selfsame being yet both spirit and flesh. Wishing to form a single creature from two levels of creation from both visible and invisible nature, says Gregory, the Creator Logos fashioned the human person. Taking a body from matter that He has previously created and placing in it the breath of life that comes from Himself, which Scripture terms the intelligent soul and the image of God, He formed *anthrōpos*, the human person, as a second universe—a great universe in a little one.

Now because we stand in this way on the crossroads of creation, because each of us, in the words of Saint Maximus the Confessor, is a laboratory or workshop that contains everything in a most comprehensive fashion, we have a special vocation, and that is to mediate and to unify.[8] Standing at the crossroads, earthly yet heavenly, body yet soul, our human vocation is to reconcile and harmonize the differing levels of reality in which we participate. Our vocation is to spiritualize the material, without thereby dematerializing it. That is why reconciliation and peace are such a fundamental aspect of our personhood.

But having said that humans are a microcosmic image of the world, we have not yet said the most important thing. The most important thing about our personhood is not that we are an image of the world, but it is that we are created in the image of God. We are a created expression of God's infinite and uncreated self-expression. Indeed Saint Gregory of Nyssa even cast scorn on the idea of a human being as the image of the world, as a microcosm. This, he says, is to glorify humans with the characteristics of the gnat and the mouse.[9] No, he says, our true glory is that we are in God's image, that we reflect the divine. Saint Maximus the Confessor develops this by saying that we are called not only to unify the different levels of the created order, but we are also called to join earth and heaven and to unite the created and the uncreated.[10]

So, made in the divine image each of us is not only *microcosmos*, but *microtheos*, a phrase used by Nicholas Berdyaev.[11] We are not only *imago mundi* but also *imago dei*—image of God. These are our two vocations—not just to unify the creation, but to offer creation back to God. As king and priest of creation formed to the image of God, the human person offers the world back to God and so transfigures it.

Now, you may have noticed that when I quoted Gregory Nazianzen, I said God formed the human person as a second universe, a great universe in a little one. But perhaps you thought, "He's got it the wrong way around, this person who persuaded the French railways to make an unscheduled stop. This triumph over the railway has gone to his head!"

But, in fact that is what Gregory said. The great universe is not the world around us, not the galaxy light years away from us. The great universe is the inner space of the heart. This is what Gregory said. We are not so much *microcosmos* as *megalocosmos*. Incomparably greater than the outside universe is the depth within each human heart.

Our vocation is not just to unify but also as *microtheos*, as image of God, it is our task to render the world transparent—diaphanic, or rather theophanic—to make God's presence shine through it.

Now if we have that kind of ideal of human personhood, what practical consequences does this have? The inner logic of the model we have been exploring surely requires a holistic view of the human person. We cannot fulfill our vocation as bridge builders, as unifiers, as cosmic priests, unless we see our own selves as a single undivided whole. More specifically, we can act as bond and mediator within the creation, rendering the material spiritual only if we see our body as an essential part of our selves, only if we view our personhood as an integral unity of body and soul. Severing our links with the material environment, we cease to mediate.

Here at once we see the very grave spiritual implications of the present pollution of the environment, what we humans are doing toward the cosmic temple that God has given us to dwell in. The fact that we are degrading the world around us in a very alarming manner shows a terrifying failure to realize our vocation as mediators. So we need, if we are to be truly human, to come to terms with our own body—with its rhythm, its mysteries, its dreams—and through our body then to come to terms with the material world.

Let us think for a little about the way in which we can and should be using our body, and let us think about how we use our bodies in worship. Christianity is a liturgical religion. Worship comes first, doctrine and moral rules come afterwards. Surely it is one of the strengths of our Orthodox Church that we still attach immense importance to symbolic action involving our body and material things. All too often in the western world people have lost the power of symbolic thinking—not entirely, but quite frequently. It is surely a deep impoverishment.

I would plead that as Orthodox Christians we should not allow ourselves to diminish the value of symbols or lose the participation of our bodies in worship. Sadly, one finds examples of such a loss. I was in the US last month and enjoyed that visit very much, but was saddened to see that many Orthodox churches have been taken over by pews. Have you reflected on the horrid effect that pews have on worship? People in pews can no longer make prostrations or even make deep bows. They just stand or sit and thus become an audience instead of active participants. In a pew it is not easy to make a proper sign of the cross with a deep bow. Now you might say that this is not so important and that pews are there for convenience and that people today just cannot stand up for very long. But traditionally the Church has provided stalls and benches on the sides or a few chairs here and there. Those who need to sit can then come forward to make prostrations. But our tradition is not one of neat rows.

Let us also take care not to diminish our Orthodox Tradition of fasting. Fasting is one way in which the body participates in prayer. Fasting is not simply the observation

of certain rigid rules and dietary restrictions. The real purpose of fasting is the renewal of prayer and of our personal
relationship with God and our fellow humans. To fast and
simply become ill-humored defeats the whole purpose of
the exercise. "What is the purpose of not eating meat," asks
Saint Basil, "if instead you devour your brother or sister?"[12]
Through fasting, through learning to do without certain
foods you take for granted, through eating more simply, we
renew the participation of our bodies. The body is the mes-
senger of the soul. The purpose of fasting is to give us freedom for prayer. Lent is a school of freedom, a season freeing
us from dependence on physical power. Indeed through
fasting we are able to see the beauty and wonder of the food
that we eat. Fasting helps us not to take food for granted.

Consider too the physical aspect of Baptism, the act of
immersion in water. Let us not diminish the materiality of
this sacramental sign. Baptism should involve the whole
body. It should represent drowning—a "joyous, devout
drench," in Philip Larkin's phrase.[13]

And let us not diminish the fact that we use bread and
wine in the Eucharist.

Let us renew for ourselves an understanding of the
sacramental value of oil in relation to healing. This may be

difficult for those coming from cultures in which olive oil is not part of daily life, as opposed to those who live in the Mediterranean. When I travel down to France and see the first olive tree, my spirit rises! I like the use of oil in our vigil service on Saturday evenings. No pilgrimage is complete unless you are anointed with oil from the lamps at the shrine. Surely we should anoint the sick with oil more than once a year, during Holy Week.[14]

I value very much the gesture of the laying on of hands. We see this in Ordination but also in our Orthodox practice of Confession. The priest confers forgiveness not from a distance but by placing his stole over the penitent and then lays his hands on the penitent's head. This is an ancient gesture associated with healing found frequently in the New Testament.

In the early period, the seventh and eighth centuries, we have evidence that this gesture took a reverse form. At the moment of absolution, the person making Confession put his hands on the neck of the priest, symbolizing that the burden was being taken away, now being carried on the shoulders of another. The priest took it on himself. It is a very serious thing to hear people's Confessions!

Another way in which the body has been diminished in western Orthodox practice in some places can be seen in modern funeral customs. When I am to preside at a funeral, I am sometimes asked not to have an open coffin. There is to be no last kiss. They prefer to see the body at the funeral parlor—not a very liturgical place! I have been told, "We couldn't do that, it would be too frightening for the children." Something has gone terribly wrong in our understanding of death if we find the body of a person whom we have loved to be somehow repellant and frightening. Surely the dead body of someone whom we love is not to be hidden away in those final hours before burial as something causing distress and disgust. Surely, we should surround the dead body with love. I am sure that children will not be frightened if our Orthodox funeral customs are properly explained. The practice of kissing the dead body is extremely ancient. We find it mentioned at least as early as the year 500 in the writings of the Dionysius the Areopagite, and perhaps the custom is far more ancient than that.[15]

So in all these ways and many others, let us give full value to our material bodies and their part in worship. "The body is divinized along with the soul," says Saint Maximus the Confessor.[16] "The flesh also is transformed," says Saint Gregory Palamas. "It is raised on high together with the soul and together with the soul it enjoys communion with God, becoming his domain and dwelling place."[17] "In the age to come," adds Palamas, "the body will share with the soul ineffable blessings."[18]

Clearly the body must share in these blessings, as far as possible, here and now.

Of the great Neoplatonist philosopher, Plotinus, it is said by his biographer Porphyry that he "was ashamed of being in the body and did not want anybody to celebrate his birthday." The occasion of his being born into this world in a body was, for him, a cause of lamentation rather than joy. He would not let anyone paint his portrait. "My appearance," he said, "is not important."[19]

But this is not the Christian attitude. I am my body and my body is me. The body is to be transfigured along with the soul. Divine grace is to be shown in and through our bodies.

In the University of London there used to be a professor of the philosophy of religion, H. G. Lewis (not to be confused with C. S. Lewis), who was much inclined, in a Platonist manner, to emphasize the contrast between body and soul. His students used to say of him that "he didn't go for a walk but rather that he took his body for a walk."

This is not the true Christian view. We are not a ghost in a machine but, on the contrary, we are called to glorify God with our body. *Your body is the temple of the Holy Spirit*, writes Saint Paul (1 Cor 6.19–20). In Romans 12 he says, *Offer your body as a living sacrifice to God*. In the words of the great prophet William Blake, "Man has no body distinct from his soul, for that called 'body' is the portion of the soul discerned by the five senses."[20]

Let me add one more comment. Our human personhood is a mystery. We do not fully understand our own selves. Sophocles observed in Antigone, "There are many strange things and none stranger than the human person."[21] Not just in our theology do we need an apophatic dimension, but we need it also in our anthropology.

Saint Gregory of Nyssa gives a specific reason for the fact that we do not understand ourselves. He connects it with the truth that the human being is made in the image and likeness of God, and the image, he says, is only truly such insofar as it expresses the attributes of the archetype. One of the characteristics of the Godhead is to be in its essence beyond our understanding. The human person is a created icon of the uncreated God, and since God is incomprehensible, so is the human person.[22]

So I ask you this evening to renew in your hearts your sense of wonder before the mystery of your own personhood. As it says in Psalm 138 [LXX], *I will praise thee, for I am fearfully and wonderfully made. Marvelous are thy works, and that my soul knoweth right well.*

2

The Passions: Enemy or Friend?

Consider the word "wonder." We have come to a place full of wonder, this ancient pilgrimage town of Vézelay. I can recall very vividly my first visit here when I was a student at university. It was in the year 1954. I was traveling with a party of fellow students in a lorry. It was from the back of that lorry that I had my first view of Vézelay—a city set on a hill—and at the heart of the summit of the city, a great church. Each time I saw Vézelay, as happened again last night when I came up from the railway station, my spirits rise, and so does my sense of wonder. I have been back ten or twelve times since 1954. Then on entering the basilica, standing in the narthex, you are faced with the marvelous sculpture of Christ in glory, which surely awakens wonder in the many pilgrims who come here.

I don't know about you, but a sense of wonder has always been very important in my reading of literature. From the age of sixteen there was one genre of Christian literature that particularly attracted me, and that was works of fantasy—for example, the stories of George McDonald. I have always enjoyed the works of fantasy by C. S. Lewis—*Out of the Silent Planet*, *Perelandra*, the Narnia books, and above all his retelling of the Psyche myth, *Till we Have Faces*.[1] Along with Lewis, I have always liked the supernatural thrillers written by his friend Charles Williams—*War in Heaven* and the rest. And there is of course Tolkien. Such stories reveal the thinness of this world, the nearness of the invisible world.

Once, when a friend of the Anglican writer Evelyn Underhill was going to Iona, her gardener said to her, "Iona is a very thin place." And she asked, "What do you mean?" The gardener, a Scotsman, said, "There is not much between Iona and the Lord." Vézelay is another thin place.

We need to be sensitive to the closeness of the invisible world. We need a sense of wonder. "The beginning of the truth is to wonder at things," said Plato.[2] That's not just Plato—it is good Christianity as well.

Have you noticed how the theme of wonder runs through Scripture? For example, in Psalm 76 [LXX] we read, *Who is so great a God as our God? Thou art the God who doest wonders.* Or take the prophesy of the incarnation in Isaiah: *For unto us a child is born . . . and his name shall be called wonderful* (Is 9.6). Throughout the Gospels we notice that the reaction of those who hear Christ's words and witness His miracles is a sense of wonder. Those who first heard the Sermon on the Mount, it is noted, *were astonished at his speech* (Mt 7.28). When Jesus rebukes the storm, we read they marveled, saying, *Who can this be?* (Mk 4.41) People met Christ with a sense of wonder. Those who heard Him teaching at the synagogue in Nazareth *were astonished* (Lk 4.32). The account of the Resurrection in Mark's Gospel reports that when the women found no body within the tomb, *they trembled and were amazed* (Mk 16.8). The Greek text says they were "seized by trauma and were ecstatic"— they were taken out of themselves with wonder. At Pentecost, when language is no longer a barrier between peoples, we find them *speaking of the wonderful works of God* (Acts 2.11). A sense of wonder is a golden thread that runs all the way through Holy Scripture. If we are to continue as faithful disciples of Christ, we need to unceasingly renew our sense of wonder.

Last night our theme was unity. Jerusalem, we are told, *is built as a city at unity with itself* (Ps 121.3, LXX). We, each one of us, must be a city at unity with ourselves. If we are to be peacemakers, we need to rediscover our inner unity. The great principle about peacemaking is from within outwards. You cannot expect peace to be imposed by governments. It must come from the human heart. From within, outwards—and we might also add from heaven, earthwards.

Our human vocation is to be *microcosmos, microtheos*—to be a mediator, to unify creation. This was the vocation given to the first Adam in paradise. Failing to fulfill it, in his fall he brought about division rather than unity. But this vocation of mediation is restored to the human race by the second Adam, Christ.

I cannot unify unless I am inwardly at one. As Saint Isaac of Syria said, "Be peaceful within yourself, and heaven and earth will be at peace with you."[3]

Now let me put before you a symbol of human unity, this complex unity of spirit, soul, and body: the symbol of the heart. What do we mean by the heart?

When the late Duchess of Windsor published her memoirs, she drew its title from a quotation by Pascal—"the heart has its reasons, which reason does not understand."[4] I confess I have not read the Duchess of Windsor's memoirs from cover to cover, but a brief consultation of that work brought home to me that by the heart, she meant the emotions and affections, perhaps somewhat disordered and wayward emotions. But that was not what Pascal meant, nor is it what Christians mean by the heart.

If we look at Scripture, we do not find in the Old or New Testament any contrast between head and heart. In the Bible, we don't just feel with our hearts—we also think with our hearts. The heart is the place of intelligence and wisdom. In Scripture, feeling and thinking are held together. In the Bible, the heart is the conscience—the moral, spiritual center of the total person. Evil thought comes from the heart, but equally the heart is where the Holy Spirit cries out, *Abba, Father* (Rom 8.15).

The heart is a unifying concept in another way. Not only does it hold together feeling and thinking, but it transcends the soul-body contrast. The heart is the spiritual organ, the center of our bodily structure, but the heart also symbolizes our spiritual understanding. It is a point of convergence and interaction for the human person as a whole.

Here is Saint Macarius of Egypt writing about the heart: "The heart governs and reigns over the whole bodily organism. And when grace possesses the pastures of the heart, it rules over all the members and the thoughts, for there in the heart is the intellect, and all thoughts of the soul and its expectations. In this way grace penetrates also to the members of the body."[5]

The heart is the center of the physical organism—when it stops beating, we are dead. But it is also the place where the intellect dwells, the center of spiritual understanding. It is through the heart that we experience grace, and through the heart grace passes to all members of the body. The heart contains, say the Macarian homilies, "unfathomable depths," including what is meant today by the unconscious.[6] There are reception rooms and bed chambers in it, doors and porches, and many offices and passages. In the heart are the works of righteousness and wickedness. In it is life; in it is death.

The heart, then, has a central and controlling role. The heart is open on one side to the unfathomable depths of the unconscious, open on the other side to the abyss of God's glory. When the Orthodox Tradition speaks of the Prayer of the Heart, that does not mean merely prayer of the feelings and emotions, it does not simply mean what in western Roman Catholic spirituality is termed affective prayer. Prayer of the Heart means prayer of the total person, prayer in which the body also participates. In the hesychast tradition, entering the heart means the total reintegration of the human person in God.

My spiritual father, Father George, once told me to read Antoine de Saint-Exupéry's *The Little Prince*. He particularly liked the words of the fox. "Now here is my secret," said the fox, "a very simple secret: It is only with the heart that one can see rightly; what is essential is invisible to the eye."[7] This is the meaning of the heart in Scripture and in the Orthodox spiritual tradition.

Now let us extend the idea of our human unity. We have said our unity as persons includes the body. But what about the passions?

In the account of the Egyptian desert given by Palladius, we read that when he went there as a young man in the fourth century, he was placed under Elder Dorotheos, who led a life of severe asceticism. He used to carry stones from one place to the other. Young Palladius thought this was excessive. "Why do you torture your body this way?" "It kills me, I kill it," Dorotheos responded.[8] But was he right? Rather than kill the body, would it not be better to transfigure the body? Another Desert Father corrected Dorotheos, saying, "We have been taught not to kill the body, but to kill the passions."[9] But should we kill the passions? Or should we transfigure them? I feel that the English poet of the seventeenth century, John Donne, comes nearer to the truth when he says, let "our affections kill us not, nor die."[10] I would agree with the seventeenth-century moralist, Sir Roger L'Estrange: "It is with our passions as with fire and water. They are good servants but bad masters."[11]

Let us explore this a little more deeply. Unfortunately, there is no satisfactory translation in English for the Greek word *pathos*. This is normally translated as "passion," sometimes as "emotion" or "affection," or it could be translated simply as suffering—the passion of Christ. There is no single English word that will convey all these different senses. It is linked to the Greek word *paschein*, which means "to suffer." So *pathos* is fundamentally a passive state. It can be regarded as something that happens to a person or object. The Greek Fathers talk about sleep and death as being *pathos,* and Gregory the Theologian describes the phases of the moon as passions. But often *pathos* actually acquires a positive sense—it is not something merely passive, it can also be something active. And so when we come across this word *pathos*, or passion, in Greek, we need to look carefully at the context, to see how it is used.

Now behind the Greek Fathers we might look at passion as it is used in Greek philosophy, especially in Aristotle.

When we read the Stoics, we find *pathos* employed in a negative sense. It means disordered impulses of the soul, an impulse that has got out of hand, that has become disobedient to reason and so is contrary to nature. As with some later Christian theologians, the passions are seen as diseases; the victim of passion is mentally deranged. For the Stoics, passions are pathological disturbances of the personality. The wise man aims at *apatheia*—dispassion, the elimination of the passions.[12] But alongside this negative view of passion, there is a more positive view in Greek philosophy. For Aristotle, the passions in themselves are neither virtues nor vices; they are neither good nor evil. We are not commended or blamed because of them. They are neutral. Everything depends on the use that we make of our passions. He includes among the passions not only such things as desire and anger, but also things such as friendship, courage, and joy.[13] So in Aristotle's view our aim should not be to eliminate the passions, but rather we should try to have a moderate and reasonable employment of them.

Plato has a similar view. He uses the famous analogy of a charioteer with a two-horse carriage.[14] The charioteer represents reason, which should be in control. One of the two horses pulling the chariot is of noble breed, the other is unruly and rebellious. And for Plato the fine horse denotes the noble emotions of the spirited part of the soul—courage, etc.—while the disorderly horse represents the baser passions of the desiring part of the soul. The implications of the analogy are clear: if the charioteer has no horses at all, the chariot is never going to get moving. It is no use simply calculating with reason; if your carriage is to get moving, you need to have a proper relationship with the other aspects of your personhood. But the analogy goes further than that. If you have a two-horse carriage and only one horse yoked to it, you won't get very far. The chariot will go askew immediately. In order for your chariot to move straight and far, you must have both horses properly harnessed, and you have to come to terms with both your horses.

So Plato's analogy is holistic—that we must all come to terms with all the different impulses in our nature if we are to live a fully human life. We cannot simply repress or ignore certain aspects of our personhood because we don't like them very much. We must learn how to use them.

Now with this twofold classical background to consider, what do we find in Christian tradition? The word *pathos* is used only three times in the New Testament: in each instance by Paul and each case in an unfavorable sense. Coming on to the Fathers, many of them take a Stoic view of the passions. Clement of Alexandria, in the early third century, regards passion as an excessive impulse disobedient to reason, contrary to nature. Passions are diseases of the soul, says Clement, and truly good persons have no passions.[15] In the fourth century, Evagrius of Pontus, disciple of the Cappadocians but also a Desert Father living the last eighteen years of his life in the Egyptian wilderness, associates the passions with demons.[16] For Evagrius, our aim is to expel the passions. The aim is *apatheia*, though Evagrius gives dispassion a positive sense, linking it with love, *agapē*.

Gregory of Nyssa takes a similar view. He says that passions were not originally part of our nature but came as a result of the Fall. For him, the passions have an animal character. They render us akin to irrational animals.[17] They express our humanity in its fallen condition.

But this is not the only view of passion in the Greek Fathers. Because it is much less well known, I would like to mention the approach of other writers who come closer to the Aristotelian view. In particular I want to look at Abba Isaiah, who lived in Egypt and then in Palestine during the fifth century. You will find a short extract from his writings in the first volume of *The Philokalia*. There is a full French translation of his writing, but it has not yet been translated into English. Abba Isaiah takes the view that desire— *epithymia*—along with envy or jealousy, anger, hatred, and pride—are all fundamentally in accordance with nature. They are not sinful, fallen distortions, but parts of our human nature as created by God.

Let me read what Abba Isaiah said: "Desire is the natural state of the intellect, because without desire for God there is no love."[18] This is also the view of John Climacus. Though he takes the negative, Stoic view of passion, when he discusses eros, he takes a more positive view.[19] He says that the erotic impulse, though it may take a sexual form and can often be distorted, can also be directed toward God. Eros is not to be eliminated but redirected, transformed. Without desire, *epithymia*, without eros, there is no proper love for God. This is why, remarks Abba Isaiah, Daniel was called *man of desire* (Dan 10.11, 19). "But the enemy twisted this into a shameful desire, a desire for every impurity."[20]

Then Abba Isaiah comes to jealousy—*zēlos* in Greek, a word that can also mean zeal. We lack an English word that conveys both senses together. There is for Abba Isaiah a zeal, a jealousy, that is "the natural state of the intellect, for without zeal there is no progress toward God."[21] Thus the Apostle Paul tells us to *strive jealously* [or, "*zealously*"] *for the good gifts* (1 Cor 12.31). He might have added that, in the Old Testament, God Himself is described as a jealous God. "However, our godly zeal has been turned into a zeal that is contrary to nature, so we are jealous, envious, and deceitful toward each other."[22]

Then he comes to anger: "Anger, too, is the natural state of the intellect, for without anger we cannot even attain purity unless we are angry toward all that which is sown in us by the enemy."[23] Again and again, in Confession I hear people telling me they have been angry, either inwardly or outwardly. I always say to them you should not simply repress your anger. If you sit on it, sooner or later it will explode. What you have to do is to use your anger in a creative way. The energy in your anger is something good, or something that can certainly be put to good use.

When anger takes a negative, destructive form, it is the misuse of something which in itself is implanted in us by God. There is ample evidence in Scripture that Christ, on various occasions, felt and showed anger. But this anger, says Abba Isaiah, "was turned against our neighbor in regard to such senseless and useless matters."[24]

Then he comes to hatred: "Likewise, hatred is the natural state of the intellect . . . for without hatred against the enemy, no honor is bestowed on the soul."[25] We are not to be like the oyster hiding quietly in its shell. My spiritual father used to say, "Even the oyster has his enemies." You need not imagine you will win people's support by doing nothing. "This hatred of ours has been twisted, however, into a state that is contrary to nature, so that we hate and loathe our neighbor, and this hatred chases away all the virtues."[26]

Then Abba Isaiah comes to pride. I wondered how he can find a good use for pride, but he does. He says:

> Similarly, a sense of pride over the enemy is the natural state of the intellect. When Job found this sense, he reproached his enemies, saying to them, *Unworthy, mean, and good-for-nothing people, whom I would not consider as worthy as the dogs in my pastures* [Job 30.1]. Yet even this interior sense of pride over our enemies

> was twisted, and, instead, we were humiliated by them,
>
> taking pride against and goading each other.[27]

What Abba Isaiah is saying here is that pride, properly understood, is a sense of our own value and meaning, and can be used as weapon against self-pity and despair, against a sense of helplessness and uselessness. But you are not useless. A sense of uselessness is not humility, but a temptation of the devil. Humility is to know that I am made in the image of God; therefore, God hopes many things from me. I have a unique vocation. Humility is to say all that I have is a gift.

In the parable of the talents, the master did not say to the servant who buried his talent and made no use of it, "Well done, you humble and modest servant. You have done much better than your proud companions who used their gift." On the contrary, the servant is rebuked who would not use his gift because he thought he was no good. So, humility is not to say I am useless, but is to say everything that I have is a gift. And pride—understood as the sense of our value and meaning in God, of our high vocation as an icon of the Holy Trinity—can be put to good use, to be used against the temptations of the devil, who says, "You are hopeless." There is a good self-love, as Saint Augustine emphasizes.[28]

When we love our true self, we can be proud of our true self. And we can be proud of our true self because our true self is in the image of the living God.

So all these things like anger and pride, which a writer in the Evagrian tradition would regard as demons, are considered by Abba Isaiah as a natural part of our personhood, created by God. Desire or anger is not in itself sinful. What matters is the way in which it is used. Our ascetic strategy is not to mortify but redirect, not eradicate but educate, not eliminate but transfigure.

It is not only Abba Isaiah who tells us that the passions can be put to good use but the later Greek Fathers. For example, Gregory Palamas talks about the "blessed passions."[29] He writes that the aim of the Christian life is not the containment of the passions but their transposition or redirection.

Again, I would commend to you the approach of John Donne: "That our affections kill us not, nor die." If we can learn to use our passions in the right way, then we should be, each of us, a true peacemaker.

3

Approaching Christ the Physician

The True Meaning of Confession and Anointing

My theme this afternoon is "Coming to Christ, the Good Physician." And I will be speaking about Confession chiefly. But I will look at it as a sacrament of healing.

In the book by Tito Colliander, *The Way of the Ascetics*, a brief conversation is recorded between a monk and a layman. The layman asks the monk, "What do you do there in the monastery?" And the monk replies, "We fall and get up, fall and get up, fall and get up again."[1] It is not only in monasteries that we do that. In a fallen and sinful world, an all-important aspect of our personhood is our need to be healed, to get up after we have fallen, our need to repent, to forgive, and to be forgiven.

We will start this afternoon with the familiar text of Saint James:

> Are any among you sick? They should call for the pres-
> byters of the church and have them pray over them,
> anointing them with oil in the name of the Lord. And
> the prayer offered in faith will save the sick, and the
> Lord will raise them up. If anyone has committed sins,
> they will be forgiven him. Therefore, confess your sins
> one to another and pray for one another so that you
> may be healed. (James 5.14–16)

What we notice in this passage is that Saint James is speaking about healing in an all-embracing sense of body and soul together. He talks about the sick person being healed through anointing with oil, but he also says that the sick person will be forgiven his sins. So, healing of body and soul go together. We are to see the human person, as we already said, in holistic terms—an undivided unity: the body is not healed apart from the soul, nor the soul apart from the body. The two are interdependent. Saint James speaks at one and the same time of the sick person being raised from his bed physically healed, and he speaks of the forgiveness of his sins through Confession. He speaks of spiritual healing.

I find this to be a key that opens a very important door, a vital clue—the Anointing of the Sick and Confession are essentially connected as two indivisible aspects of a single mystery of healing and forgiveness. Each has its own specific function—they do not replace one another, but together they form a true union. So, perhaps the most helpful way to look at the sacrament of Confession is to see it as a sacrament of healing.

Now, sacramental Confession as we know it today in the Orthodox Church represents a convergence of two things that originally were, perhaps, distinct. First of all, there is the administration of penance. This is particularly connected with John, chapter 20, verses 22 through 23. There, the risen Christ breathes on His disciples, confers on them the gift of the Holy Spirit, and He says, *Whosoever sins you forgive, they are forgiven; whosoever sins you retain, they are retained.*

There, the risen Christ gives to His disciples the power of binding and loosing sins—a juridical power. This task of binding and loosing was transmitted from the apostles to their successors, the bishops. In the early Church the administration of penance was something public; it did not involve the private giving of counsel or advice. It was something exceptional. You hoped, by God's mercy, that you would not have to be involved in penance. Indeed, the penances that were imposed were by our standards extremely severe. It often requires a leap of the imagination on our part to think of how life was in the ancient Church. For example, for fornication—I mean, sex outside of marriage—Saint Gregory of Nyssa assigns a penance of nine years without Communion.[2] Saint Basil's a little more merciful—he says seven years without Communion.[3] Finally, in the sixth and seventh century, in the canonical legislation of Saint John the Faster, it is reduced to two years.[4] Even so, by our standard, that may well seem severe. Does any part of the Orthodox Church today impose penances of that kind?

Another example is involuntary manslaughter—for example, killing somebody in a car accident. In the early Church the act of accidental killing of another person meant ten years without Communion. Perhaps, says Saint John the Faster, if you observe strict fasting, it can be reduced to three years. Parents who allow a child to die unbaptized—three years without Communion.[5] So it continues.

Now, that is one source of Confession as we know it—the system of public penance that existed in the early Church. But this is seen as something exceptional, not a regular part of people's Christian life—only if they got into trouble. It was not primarily a question of spiritual direction.

But then there is another source of the sacrament of Confession as we know it today. This is the practice of spiritual counsel, first found especially in the Egyptian monasticism of the fourth century, though no doubt the practice of using spiritual counsel goes right back to apostolic times. But we do not know very much about it until the emergence of monasticism.

In the desert of Egypt, as we have learned from the *Gerontikon* and the *Apophthegmata*—or *Sayings of the Desert Fathers*—an important part was played by the disclosure of thoughts. The disciple would go perhaps daily to his spiritual elder, his *staretz*, and open his heart to him. Now this is something clearly different from the system of public penance. First of all, it is regular, not exceptional. In many monastic centers, this happens daily. Second, it is private, not public. It is carried out under conditions of confidentiality. It does not directly involve the church hierarchy.

The spiritual father—in a monastic context, the elder—may in fact be a layman, not a priest. Anthony of Egypt was never a priest but he formed in many ways the prototype of the monastic spiritual father. Athanasius calls him a

physician given by God to all of Egypt. The spiritual father of
Saint Simeon the New Theologian of the eleventh century—
Simeon the Studite—was not a priest. Saint Silouan of
Mount Athos was not a priest. On the Holy Mountain today
there are many spiritual fathers who are lay monks. Indeed,
the giving of spiritual counsel can surely be done by a lay
Christian—a man or woman—a person not in monastic
vows at all, though that is more exceptional.

In this practice of spiritual counsel, the scope is far
wider than in the formal penance of the Church. What
you disclose to your elder is not just your sins, but your
thoughts. You don't only speak of what you've done wrong,
you share with him your inner state, your whole situation.
The hope is that by revealing your thoughts to your elder,
you will in fact avoid falling into sin. In other words, penance is retrospective, picking up the pieces after the breakage; but, through the use of spiritual counsel, you hope to
avoid the breakage itself.

When I was a student at Magdalen College in Oxford,
there was a formidable guardian of the chapel, the verger, a
little man called Tallboy. I remember a new dean of Divinity
arrived and, with some severity, Tallboy explained to him
all the traditions and practices of the college chapel. At the

end of this, the new dean of Divinity said, a little nervously, "Thank you, Mr Tallboy; you put me right when I go wrong." "Sir," said Tallboy, "I'll put you right before you go wrong."

Now, the first law of penance puts you right after you have gone wrong, but the first law of the disclosure of thoughts, so one hopes, puts you right before you have gone wrong.

The underlying principle behind this monastic disclosure of thoughts is very clear; it is described in this way in the *Gerontikon*, a collection of sayings of the Desert Fathers: If impure thoughts trouble you, do not hide them, but tell them at once to your spiritual father and condemn them. The more a person conceals his thoughts, the more they multiply and gain strength. But an evil thought, when revealed, is immediately destroyed. If you hide things, they have great power over you, but if you could only speak of them before God, in the presence of another, then they will often wither away, and lose their power.

The process of bringing into the open what is hidden is decisive behind spiritual counsel. That, of course, is also the principle in modern psychotherapy, but the Desert Fathers thought of it before Freud and Jung.

If, in the first place, public penance is a primarily juridical model, in the second case, spiritual counsel is a more therapeutic model. Confession as we know it today represents a growing together of these two tendencies. From the fourth century onward, with the greatly increased number of Christians, the system of public penance fell increasingly into disuse. In a much larger Christian community, the trust that existed in the first centuries of the Church was diluted. To discuss publicly, in the presence of the whole community, the sins of individual members became a cause of scandal. And so from the fourth century onward, increasingly penance is no longer public. It becomes a personal meeting with the bishop alone and the one who has fallen into sin. Also, with the increasing number of Christians, the bishop could not possibly administer the practice of penance on his own, so he delegates this task to specific priests.

Up until the present day in the Greek Church still only a minority of priests hear Confessions. This is not something conferred automatically at Ordination. There is a special ceremony in the *Euchologion*—the book of prayers—for the appointment of a priest as a confessor and spiritual father. Generally, in Greek tradition, priests do not hear Confession until they have received that special blessing from the bishop.

Once Confession and the practice of penance became private, then probably the priest appointed to deal with this matter would not limit himself simply to imposing a penance, but he would offer some kind of guidance, some kind of healing counsel. So, increasingly the administration of penance from the fourth century onward takes in elements from the second strand I was describing, the tradition of spiritual counsel.

But there has never been a complete fusing between the two. The practice, as I have already said, of people going to a monk who is not a priest for counsel and to ask God's forgiveness, has not entirely ceased.

Now, in our view of Confession today, where do we put the primary emphasis? Do we put it mainly on the aspect of penance, or on the aspect of spiritual counsel? Do we think of Confession primarily in juridical terms, as coming to Christ as the Judge? Do we think of it, on the other hand, more in therapeutic terms, as coming to Christ as the Good Physician, the Doctor? Do we see sin primarily as the breaking of the Law, in medieval terms, or do we see sin more as the symptom of inner illness? Do we emphasize mainly binding and loosing—or healing? Is coming to Confession like going to a law court, or like going to a hospital?

Now, our answer surely should be, there is truth in both approaches. They are not mutually exclusive.

I remember when I first traveled to America as a hungry student, I went by boat. In those days—the 1950s—air travel was extremely expensive. It was only for the wealthy. So, unless you were rich, you went for five days on one of the great ocean liners. I can recall traveling on the liner, the Queen Elizabeth. The price of the meals was included in your ticket. I was delighted to find on my birthday that on the menu there was a huge list of food, and you did not have to choose just one item out of three courses. You could make as many courses as you liked. At breakfast, you didn't have to have either fruit juice or cereal or porridge, you could have all three. You could then go on to have both fried eggs and poached haddock, if you felt like that in the heaving waters of the mid-Atlantic. At dinner the other people at my table were very small-minded. They just had soup and then a main course and then pudding. But I worked it out that I could have hors d'oeuvres and melon, soup, fish, meat, and then dessert, then fruit and then cheese. It wasn't a question of either/or, but it could be both/and.

Now I would suggest spiritually we should follow the path of the luxury liner! We should not assume that we must think of Confession either in legalistic terms or in terms of healing; rather we should combine the two. Even so I have to say that I myself find the therapeutic model much more helpful—to see Confession above all as a sacrament of healing, to think of it as coming to Christ the Doctor. The priest is not the doctor; he is the medical assistant. If you are given a penance, it is not a punishment, it is a tonic to help you recover afterward, to get better.

Of course, this means if you do have a therapeutic approach to Confession that you need more time, you cannot just deal with things in two minutes. In my experience, though I am in a fairly small parish, I find I need a quarter of an hour on average for each Confession, but during Lent we might spend considerably longer, even a whole hour, together.

If you stress the element of healing, Confession is less troubling. It is a time for a true opening of hearts.

What we bring to Christ is not a laundry list of sins, but we bring ourselves. We bring not just our sins, but our sinfulness, because often there is a sinfulness that is far deeper than the specific acts we mention. But again, we do not isolate our sinfulness from our total personhood. What we bring to Christ in Confession is ourselves, and we may need time to do that.

If we think of Confession in terms of healing, we also have to remember that healing takes time. Normally it doesn't happen suddenly. We should never think of each Confession in an isolated way, separately from all the others. We should recognize that Confession is a process as well as an event. In going to a series of Confessions, if possible to the same priest, gradually we change, even though we may feel that nothing very remarkable happened at any specific Confession. Yet over time we realize, yes, we have been healed.

How many of Christ's parables in the Gospels speak of slow, gentle, secret growth, unseen by us but seen by God? Think, for example, of Mark 4.26–29. This is one of the very few passages that is only in Mark, and not in any of the other Gospels. And Mark, speaking there of the harvest, says that you were first the blade, the tender stalk, then you have the ear, or head. And then gradually the full corn in the ear, the head full of grain, but it happens very slowly, and we do not see it happening, though after time we notice the difference. Is that not true, very often, of our own spiritual lives? Certainly, it was true of Mark himself, who got off to a rather shaky start. Paul was displeased with him and would not take him on his second missionary journey. But at the end of his life, Paul writes to Timothy, *Get Mark and bring him with you, for he is useful to me for ministry* (2 Tim 4.11), so evidently Mark made progress.

Christ Himself recognizes how long and drawn out the process of forgiveness may be. We have to forgive people to *seventy times seven* (Mt 18.22). That is often what God has to do to us. We should not feel discouraged if we have to keep mentioning the same sin over and over again at successive Confessions. Does that mean that the Confession is useless? Does it mean that we are just wasting our own time and the priest's time? Not necessarily. When we feel, "Well, I can't go to Confession because I'd only have the same things to say"—that is a temptation of the devil. We must go back. We must keep mentioning these things. Change happens slowly.

Throwing together what I have been saying about Confession, I would like to ask the question: Why go to Confession at all? If, after I have sinned, I turn to God in prayer and, with all sincerity of heart, I ask Him to forgive me, saying my evening prayers that day, does not God at once forgive my sin? Why, then, do I need to go to Confession?

My answer is, yes, God does forgive my sin when I confess it in full sincerity of heart from that very moment, but we still need to go to Confession for several reasons. In Confession, there are basically three of us there: there is me, making my Confession; there is the priest, listening as witness; and there is God—Christ the Physician—who forgives and heals.

Let us consider what each of these three people do.

First of all, there is what I do. Earlier I quoted from the *Sayings of the Desert Fathers*—if a thought is concealed, repressed, hidden within us, it has great power. But if we can only bring it into the open, it loses its power over us. Now there is the first reason to go to Confession. Yes, I can confess my sins alone in my evening prayer, but there is great power in the uttered word. If I externalize this, if I bring them into the open, what has hitherto been internal, perhaps only half-conscious, now assumes an objective existence, and so I can deal with it. Let us not underestimate the effect upon us of speaking about our secret thoughts and sins.

As part of our church service, the mystery of Confession in the presence of another person deepens. Often, it is surprising how in Confession itself, we say things that we did not realize lay in our power to say. Sometimes in Confession itself, our whole situation becomes clear as we speak. We did not really know what we were going to say until we said it. In this way, the process of speaking can have a creative impact.

Of course, we are to prepare before Confession. People who are afraid that because of the erratic character of human memory, or because of nervousness, they may forget things—yes, certainly they may write a few things down on paper. I always discourage people from writing their whole Confession down before they come to simply read from a piece of paper what is there. The creative work of putting it into words needs to happen in the Confession itself. The same is true, mind you, of preaching sermons. Certainly, we should prepare: it is not advisable to just get up and say the first thing that comes into your head. That, on the whole, won't really help people. You should have a clear notion before we begin our sermon of what the theme is going to be, what is going to proceed from the point, and we may even have something written down. But we should not read a prepared statement word-for-word. When that is done, it means that the creative work was done in our study, perhaps several days before, and what we are offering to the congregation is merely the cold ashes afterward. That is a little harsh, but it wasn't I who said that. I think it was Saint Ignatius Brianchaninov. The same is true of Confession:

make a few notes if you wish, but always find the words at the actual moment of Confession. So the creative work is happening in the Confession itself.

That ends the first point—what I do, the power of the uttered word. Then there is what the priest does. Here I think there are two points—one more obvious, the other perhaps less so. The obvious thing is that the priest can give us counsel, advice. Many people think that is the main reason for going to Confession. Actually, I would say, what I—the penitent—do is more important than the advice the priest gives me. But nonetheless, the priest's advice can be decisive.

It is a remarkable thing, there are statements that, if you read them printed in a book, would not strike you as in any way remarkable. You might say, "Well, that's obvious enough!" But when the same words are spoken to you by the priest hearing your Confession, they may suddenly prove to be words of fire. Words that, taken in the abstract, may seem very ordinary and simple, in Confession may suddenly come alive. If you are receptive, they may alter your life.

I remember one case. At the Russian convent in London to which I often went as a layman, there was an elderly priest, Father John, who did not like preaching sermons and did not like hearing Confessions. He was always extremely laconic. Few words of advice were given. One day, a woman who often came to him for Confession told him as usual and at great length the arguments that she had had with her husband. "He said this and I said this and then he said this and I told him he was all wrong and said this and this and this . . ." At the end of all this, Father John simply looked at her, and said, "And did it help?" Then he gave her absolution.

Those four words changed her life. She suddenly saw how futile it was to go on arguing all the time, always trying to answer people back, always wanting to have the last word. She suddenly thought, "It doesn't have to be like that at all." She stopped it and changed. It was that very simple word of advice from the priest, put in the form of a question, that made her life different.

I remember a friend of mine who went to one of the Greek priests in the cathedral. She was a little taken aback—indeed, a little offended at first—because his advice was limited to five words. He just said: "Not serious, but too many," and then gave her absolution. Again, that made a difference. It altered her attitude toward herself.

When in Confession, listen very carefully to what the priest says. He is not simply offering general advice, reflections on the human predicament. He is speaking to me, calling on the Holy Spirit to guide him. What are these words from the Spirit that the priest has to say to me here and now? If we will really listen, then we shall learn.

I remember going one day to a Russian church when I was a layman, wanting to go to Confession, and asking, "Which one of the priests speaks English?" I was told, "Go to that one." So I did. Once I had confessed, he began talking to me, but I could not understand a word. So I said, "Could you please speak English?" And he said in an irritated voice, "I am speaking English!" It was not a promising beginning for our mutual cooperation!

So even though what I do may be more important than what the priest does, yet the priest's counsel can often change my life, if I will let it do so. We must not expect the priest to do everything. When Christ was among people with no faith, he could not work any miracles there. It is always two-sided. If I, the penitent or the disciple, am not receptive, then the spiritual father will not have a healing word for me.

There is another way in which the priest's role is important, which, perhaps, we forget. The priest is there as the representative of the church community. Penance, as we saw earlier, was originally a public event. All the local community were there. Now it is personal and private, but the priest is nonetheless representing the community. There are no entirely private sins. All sins are sins against my neighbor, as well as against God and against myself. Even my most secret thoughts are, in fact, making it more difficult for those around me to follow Christ.

All personal sins have a negative effect on other persons, though they may not be consciously aware they do. So, when I come to Confession, I come to ask forgiveness not only from God, but also from my sisters and brothers, from the community. I see the priest, therefore, who is present as a witness, as the representative of the community.

Let me give an example. I have heard this story twice, told by quite different people. Perhaps it happened twice. This is a story involving someone I had the privilege of meeting personally and knowing, a saint of our Church, Saint John Maximovitch, who was a bishop of Shanghai, then here in France, then finally San Francisco.

Once, a man was making Confession to him, and he said to Archbishop John, "Yes, I see that I have sinned. With my mind, I appreciate that what I have done is wrong, but my heart is like a stone—I feel no sense of sorrow or compunction." Now, the Confession was being heard just before the Liturgy and there were already many people in the church. Archbishop John said to the man, "Go out into the middle of the church, kneel in front of all these people, and ask their forgiveness, and then come back to me."

The man did so. And when he knelt before the people and asked their forgiveness, a sudden change occurred inside him. Suddenly, the stoniness of his heart was taken away. Suddenly, something that held back his tears of compunction was released, and he was able to weep over his sin, and then he received absolution. This brings out the importance of the priest as a representative of the community. We have to ask forgiveness of our fellow Christians.

Here I would join Father Alexander Men in issuing a word of caution. There is, in my view, a great danger of over-emphasizing the role of the spiritual father. People read Dostoevsky's account of Staretz Zosima,[6] which is indeed a marvelous piece of writing, and then they think, "That's how it's going to be for me. I'm going to find a spiritual father who will know all my thoughts before I confess them; who will alter my life with a single healing word." Now, for many of us, that is not the way things happen.

Priests have to be very careful, if they are in a parish and are hearing Confessions of married couples, not to demand of lay people the kind of obedience that is appropriate only in a monastery. There is a danger sometimes of parish priests thinking, "I shall be Saint Seraphim; I shall be Staretz Zosima." But even in a monastery, those kinds of spiritual fathers are very much the exception. We should not, as priests, be too quick to claim the authority of a charismatic staretz. Perhaps I am a Saint Seraphim, perhaps I am not.

So I would see the primary purpose of the spiritual father—especially among lay people, but it applies also in monasteries—is to help others to discover their freedom. Not to tell them what they should do, but to help them, through the use of their own freedom, to stand with their own conscience before God and to come to an informed decision.

Very often people come to a spiritual father wanting him to make the decision for them, and perhaps the answer is they have to make the decision. The spiritual father can help them to see what the issue is.

I recall Father Sophrony [now Saint Sophrony—*Ed.*] telling me about the approach of Saint Silouan of Mount

Athos toward those who came to him. He said Staretz
Silouan hardly ever told people exactly what to do; he
hardly ever issued commands. Much more often, he would
ask them questions—very carefully chosen questions, yes—
but he did not issue orders. He wanted people to think for
themselves. Father Sophrony said that if Staretz Silouan did
give counsel in a more detailed way, he frequently began
his sentences with the word, "If." In other words, he tried
to help people see connections, to see that if they did one
thing, then that would lead on to something else, so there
is a chain of cause and effect within our spiritual lives. He
tried to help people see how things hang together, how one
thing leads to another. Still, he left it to them to make up
their own minds.

If somebody comes to me and just says, "Tell me what
I should do," my response is, "That is not the real question.
You can only discover what you should do if you look in
a much more precise way at what the possibilities are, and
what the alternatives are. Then you can begin to make a
choice. But the question, just in the abstract, 'What should I
do?' is not yet ready for an answer." The spiritual father does
not issue orders; he is not a lawgiver. We hear this again and

again in the *Sayings of the Desert Fathers*. But he can, some-times, help people to see what the question is.

The purpose of Confession is that it is a school for heal-ing. I mentioned what I do in Confession and what the priest does. Thirdly, there is what God does, and that is, by far, the most important thing of all.

Confession is a sacrament, a mystery. Divine grace is at work in it. Confession, like all the other sacraments, is God's action in which we, both penitent and priest, are invited to share.

What Saint John Chrysostom says of the Divine Lit-urgy is true also of Confession. Of the Liturgy, Saint John Chrysostom says, "The priest only lends his hand and provides his tongue. Everything is brought to pass by the Father, the Son, and the Holy Spirit."[7] When the priest in Confession lays his stole on the head of the penitent and then his hand upon the penitent's head, it is the hand of Christ he lays upon him. That is made very clear in the exhortation at the beginning of the Russian rite of Confes-sion: "Christ stands invisibly before us, I am only a witness, bearing testimony before Him of all the things you have to say to me."

So here you have my reasons for suggesting that is why we do need to go to Confession.

Let me end with a quotation not from an Orthodox writer but from a Protestant, a Lutheran, Dietrich Bonhoeffer. Speaking of Confession, he says, "Who can refuse, without suffering loss, the help that God has thought it necessary to offer us?"[8]

4

"In Peace Let Us Pray to the Lord"

Peace and Healing in the Divine Liturgy

This afternoon I spoke about the sacrament of Confession. Tonight, I would like to say something about the Holy Eucharist.

Let me begin with two words. The first is from nineteenth-century Russia, Saint John of Kronstadt: "The Eucharist is a continual miracle."[1] And my second word is from fourteenth-century Byzantium, from Saint Nicolas Cabasilas: "This is the final mystery. Beyond this it is not possible to go, nor can anything be added to it."[2] So, let us reflect together this evening on this "continual miracle," this "final mystery," which holds the Church in unity, makes the Church to be itself, and which is the heart of our life as Christians.

I would like to look at two things: first, "What is the meaning of the word *liturgy*?" and second, "How do we speak about *peace* during the course of the Liturgy?"

First of all, what is the meaning of the word "liturgy," the word that the Orthodox use above all when referring to the service of Holy Communion? The Greek term *leitourgia* is sometimes explained as meaning the "work of the people." That, I am told, is bad etymology, but it is, in fact, quite good theology, because liturgy indeed means precisely a shared, corporate action. Liturgy is something done by many persons in common, something that none of us can do alone. So, if the Eucharist is termed liturgy, that means that, at the service, there are only active participants, there are no passive spectators.

Let us think together about the way in which the corporate, shared nature of the Divine Liturgy is expressed. Throughout the service, except on rare occasions, all the prayers use the plural, not the singular. We say throughout the Liturgy "we," not "I." Exceptions are only apparent exceptions. At the beginning of the Creed, it is true, it starts "I believe." That is because the Creed was originally used in the service of Baptism, and so the person being baptized as an adult used the singular when making his or her profession of faith. When the Creed was introduced from the Baptismal Service into the Divine Liturgy, the singular was preserved. If you look at the prayer said before the Great Entrance by the priest during the Hymn of the Cherubim, again you will see that he uses the word "I," but that is a prayer said secretly by the priest. It was never said aloud. It was introduced into the Liturgy at a time after the prayers had come to be said in a low voice so that they could not be heard by the people. As it is a priest's prayer, it naturally fits to say "I." Equally, in the Russian use, before Communion we use the prayer "I believe, O Lord, and I confess," but that really belongs to the Prayers of Preparation, not to the Liturgy itself, and so, naturally, when a person is saying the Prayers of Preparation alone in his or her own room, it is appropriate for him or her to say, "I believe and I confess."

Elsewhere in the Liturgy, the word used is "we." And in this way the Liturgy reflects the pattern of prayer given to us by our Lord Jesus Christ: the Lord's Prayer. In the Lord's Prayer we say "us" five times, "our" three times, "we" once; but never at all do we say in the Lord's Prayer, "me," "mine,"

or "I." So, the liturgical pronoun is "we," not "I." And that
underlines that the Liturgy is a common, shared act.

I often think of the story retold by Dostoevsky in *The
Brothers Karamazov* about an old woman and an onion.[3]
You will all know it—how the angel tried to pull her out of
the lake of fire, and how the other people in the lake of fire
climb on in the hope of being pulled out as well, and how
the old woman, alarmed by this, cried out, "Let go. Let go.
It is not you who are being pulled out. It's me. It's not your
onion; it's mine." And as we know, when she said, "It's mine,"
the onion snapped in two, and she fell back into the lake of
fire. And there, so I am told, she still is. If only she said,
"It is our onion," surely the onion would have been strong
enough to have pulled them all out together. In saying, "It is
my onion," she was being profoundly un-liturgical; indeed,
she was denying her human personhood.

As persons made in the image of God, we are made
in the image of God the Holy Trinity; and the Holy Trinity signifies mutual love. If we are made in the image of the
Trinity, that means we are made to love one another. And if
we refuse to love one another, that means we lose our true
human personhood. So, there is no true person unless there
are at least two persons—better still, three—in dialogue with

one another. The doctrine of the Trinity means, in terms of our human personhood, I need you in order to be myself.

So that is the first way in which we see how the Liturgy is always a shared action. Always we say "we." The Liturgy expresses mutual love. One of the things that I was taught by Nicholas Zernov very early in my acquaintance with the Orthodox Church was how important in the Liturgy is the phrase "Let us love one another, that with one mind we may confess: Father, Son, and Holy Spirit—the Trinity, one in essence and undivided." Without mutual love there is no true confession of the Trinity, and no true Liturgy. I remember when I first became a priest in Oxford, Nicholas said to me, "We must have that portion of the Liturgy in English." He was very keen on having everything in English, if possible. This was not the view of all the other people in the parish, but evidently he thought the English speakers especially needed to be reminded of mutual love. What a pity, in most of our Orthodox Churches, we do not exchange the kiss of peace among the congregation at that point. I don't know what you do here in Vézelay. You have the kiss of peace? Well, I would expect nothing less of Father Stephen, but I am afraid that we do not at Oxford, and that is a sad thing, though the exchange of the kiss of peace among the congregation had already dropped out quite early. By the time of Saint Maximus it was only being exchanged among the clergy.

As we continue talking about "we," let us notice another element in the Liturgy that stresses the importance of mutual love, the importance of communal solidarity at the service. When, as celebrant, I come into the church for the start of the service, before I go into the sanctuary to put on my vestments, I say the Prayers of Preparation in front of the iconostasis. I then venerate the icons. I then turn to the west, away from the sanctuary, and bow. Often nobody else has arrived in the church at that time, so I only bow to the angels, but if there are people there as well, then they should bow back. A second time, before I go as the celebrant to the Holy Table to take the gifts of bread and wine and carry them in the procession of the Great Entrance, once more I bow to the people, and they bow back. A third time, before Holy Communion, once more the celebrant turns and bows to the people, and they bow back, though in most Orthodox churches at this moment, the doors are closed and the curtain is drawn, so nobody sees that.

What are we doing when we exchange these bows with each other? Is this simply a mutual courtesy? No, it has a far more specific meaning. The priest, as he bows, says aloud, or else in his heart, "Forgive me." And the people, when they bow back, and respond, either aloud or in their heart, in the same way: "Forgive us." And each may say in their heart, "May God forgive us." So what we are doing in the exchange of bows is giving and receiving pardon—mutual forgiveness. And this, again, shows how in the Eucharist we never come to receive Communion alone as isolated individuals. We come as members of a community; and, we come, or we should come, as members of a reconciled community—a community that is at peace with itself. Without the giving and receiving of forgiveness, there is no true celebration in the full sense.

Then, third, let us note another thing in the Liturgy. Before the beginning of the Anaphora, the great prayer of offering, there is an opening dialogue. The celebrant or deacon says, "Let us stand aright, let us stand with fear." Then the people respond, in the correct text, "Mercy, peace, a sacrifice of praise." In fact, in most churches they say, "a mercy of peace," but that does not make very good sense. If we consult the older Greek manuscripts we find, "Mercy, peace, a sacrifice of praise."

Notice that we begin by speaking of peace before we begin the Great Prayer. Then the celebrant blesses the people, "The grace of our Lord Jesus Christ, the love of God the Father, and the communion of the Holy Spirit be with you all." The people respond: "And with your spirit." "Let us lift up our hearts." The people answer, "We lift them up unto the Lord." "Let us give thanks to Lord." The people answer, "It is meet and right." Incidentally, if we followed the more ancient texts, we should not go on by singing, "It is meet and right to worship the Father, and the Son, and the Holy Spirit, the Trinity one in essence" and so on. The meaning of the people's response is. "It is meet and right to give thanks," and so it remains in the Greek tradition, but the Russians added other words in order to fill up space while the priest was saying the prayer silently. If you say the prayers aloud, there is no need to do that. It actually obscures the meaning of the people's response there. (We need quite a lot of liturgical tidying up in our Orthodox churches, but this is the proper critical text of the Liturgy based on the best manuscripts. Perhaps that is something we might get on with as Orthodox in a constructive way instead of arguing about other matters.)

Now what is the meaning of this opening dialogue? Here is the explanation given by Saint John Chrysostom in his commentary on the Second Epistle to the Corinthians:

As we begin the actual celebration of the dread mysteries, the priest prays for the people and the people pray for the priest, for the words "and with thy spirit" mean precisely this: Everything in the eucharistic thanksgiving is shared in common. For the priest does not offer thanksgiving alone, but the whole people give thanks with him. For after he has replied to their greeting, they then give their consent by answering: "It is meet and right." Only then does he begin the eucharistic thanksgiving.[4]

So as Saint John Chrysostom understands it, this opening dialogue exactly expresses our togetherness as we embark upon the central part of the Eucharist. The priest alone says the prayer of the Anaphora, but the people are directly and actively involved in everything that he does. And so, in this dialogue, the unity of priest and people in the shared action of the Liturgy is clearly underlined. The priest greets the people, "The grace of our Lord Jesus Christ . . ." and they respond to his greeting, "And with thy spirit." This is mutual prayer, as Saint John Chrysostom explains it. The priest then invites the people to raise their hearts on high; and the people respond by saying, "That is exactly what we're doing!" And then the priest says, "Let us give thanks to the Lord," and that could also be translated: "Let us offer the Eucharist to the Lord." And the people say, "That is an excellent idea." Only when they have responded in that way does the celebrant continue. The celebrant is, as it were, asking permission from the people to continue with the eucharistic celebration. He needs their endorsement. He cannot act on his own. The prayer is theirs as well as his. Their active consent is indispensable. So the eucharistic Anaphora begins with a dialogue because the Eucharist is, par excellence, the human action. We are eucharistic animals as human beings; and also, the human animal is essentially a dialogic animal—an animal that engages in dialogue. So what that dialogue before the Anaphora is expressing is just what I said a few minutes ago: I need you in order to be myself.

All of this then helps us to understand how the Eucharist, if it is to be properly celebrated, needs to be celebrated by a community that is at least at unity within itself. It is offered by nobody singly, but by all of us in loving fellowship with one another. That is the ideal. Let us all try to make it also the reality.

Now I would like to move to my second point, which concerns the meaning of the word "peace." This is a recurrent phrase in the Liturgy: peace. Here I borrow from the excellent little book by the Monk of the Eastern Church, Father Lev Gillet, *Serve the Lord With Gladness*.[5] Father Lev has a great gift for expressing deep truths with remarkable conciseness and simplicity.

[*Met. Kallistos made a gesture imitating quotations marks, then explained:*] There was a minister in America some years ago who used to begin and end all of his sermons with a gesture like this. People asked him, "Why do you do that?" "My sermons," he replied, "are not my own. They are actually taken from other people, and those are the quotation marks." So for this little bit, as I am paraphrasing Father Lev, I ought to do this as well.

Let us reflect for a moment on the text of the Great Litany at the beginning of the service, the Litany of Peace. Three times we speak about peace: "In peace let us pray to the Lord"; "For the peace from above and for the salvation of our souls, let us pray to the Lord"; "For the peace of the whole world and the good estate of the holy churches of God and for the communion of all, let us pray to the Lord."

This threefold request for peace is not a superfluous repetition. Each repetition is charged with a distinctive significance.

At the very outset of the public part of the Liturgy, we establish the fact that peace is the spiritual space in which the Divine Liturgy is being celebrated. We start by saying, "In peace, let us pray to the Lord." We cannot enter into the action of the Liturgy or experience the joy of the Kingdom unless we have within our hearts, by God's mercy, a state of interior peace. So we start by seeing peace as an inner state of our soul: "In peace"—the state of wholeness and of integration. So at the beginning of the Liturgy we are to banish, from within ourselves, feelings of resentment and hostility toward others: bitterness, rancor, inner grumbling, or divisiveness. We are to shed these things; let them go; begin the Liturgy "in peace." That is Stage I.

Then Stage II: "For the peace from above . . ." Peace is not just a psychological state produced by my own effort. Peace, true peace, comes from above as a gift from God, a gift of grace. *Without me,* says Christ, *you can do nothing* (Jn 15.5). In translating *The Philokalia,* I have been struck by the surprising frequency with which that text is quoted. *Without me you can do nothing.* We see that peace is not a manufactured article, something manmade. It is a gift, a charisma. We therefore have to open our hearts to receive Christ's gift of peace: "the peace from above." As it says in Ephesians

2.14, *He is our peace.* Notice in this second petition how peace is closely joined with salvation: "For the peace from above and for the salvation of our souls." Salvation, in the tradition of the Christian East, is not understood primarily in juridical terms, as a release from guilt, although it is that in part. But salvation thought of positively means whole- ness, fullness of life. We cannot have that wholeness, that fullness of life, without the divine gift of peace.

Then we come to the third petition: "For the peace of the whole world, the good estate of the holy churches of God, the union of all." The peace that we seek is not just inward looking, not world-denying. It is outward going, active, practical. We seek peace not for myself alone, but for and with others. If I seek peace selfishly, I will not find it. Peace and unity go together.

So then, that is the sequence: "in peace"—"peace from above"—"peace of the whole world." Peace is not self- centered. It is outward looking, ecstatic (in the literal sense of that word), generous, and practical.[6] In Father Lev's words, "We pray for the peace of the universe. Not only for humans, but for all creatures: for animals, for vegetables, for stars, for the whole of nature."[7] So we enter into a cosmic piety. We express our sympathy with everything to which

God has given being. But though our prayer for peace is not limited to the human race, that is certainly where we begin. And how urgent at all times, but especially now, is the need for the prayer begging Christ to give peace to this suffering world.

Then we have God's response to that threefold prayer for peace. It comes a little later in the service when the celebrant says to the congregation, "Peace be with all." In Slav use, that is said soon after the Little Entrance and the Trisagion. In Greek use and, again, in the Slav, it comes before the Gospel, and repeatedly thereafter. "Peace be unto all." That is not just an empty phrase but is a powerful performative utterance—not just a courteous formality, but the transmission of a reality. Now what the priest is transmitting is not his own peace. He is speaking at this moment in Christ's name. He is transmitting to the people God's peace: *The peace of God which passes all understanding* (Phil 4.7) We think at this point of Christ's words at the Last Supper: *My peace I give to you. Not as the world gives, give I unto you* (Jn 14.27). There is a two-way traffic. Our prayer for peace is the one movement, then the responding movement, God's gift of peace. The effect of peace is unity with ourselves; unity with God; unity with others around us. Peace and unity in this way are essential marks of the eucharistic celebration.

So then, remembering Plato's words—"The beginning of truth is to wonder at things"—I ask you tonight to renew your sense of wonder before the final mystery, the great mystery of the Eucharist. I began with the words of Saint John of Kronstadt, who was a very profoundly eucharistic priest, so let me end with his words: "In the words 'take, eat, drink' there is contained the abyss of God's love for humankind. O perfect Love! O all-embracing Love! O irresistible Love! What shall we give to God in gratitude for this Love?"[8]

5

"Let Us Go Forth in Peace"

Healing in the Parish, in the Local Church, and in the World

Our theme is the liturgy after the Liturgy.

I am reminded of Tolstoy's story, called "The Three Hermits."[1] Do you know it?

Once upon a time there was a bishop traveling from Arkhangelsk to the Solovetsky Islands on the White Sea. And in the middle of the morning, the captain pointed out to him an apparently deserted island, and he said, "It's very interesting. There are three hermits on that island." "Let's turn aside," said the bishop, "and go and meet them."

So the boat turned aside, and sure enough as they drew in toward the shore, they saw three old men standing hand in hand with long white beards. And so the bishop got down from the boat and landed on the shore, and he bowed deep to the holy men and said, "Pray for me." And the three hermits bowed deep and said, "Holy bishop, bless us."

"How do you pray, holy men?" asked the bishop.

The hermits replied, "This is how we pray: 'Three are we, three are ye, have mercy on us.'"

"Oh," said the bishop, "that is not actually the right way to pray. Do you know the Lord's Prayer?"

"No," they said, "we've never heard of that prayer."

"Alright," said the bishop, "I'll teach you the Lord's Prayer."

So he told them the Lord's Prayer, and he tried to get them to learn it by heart. The three old men were very anxious to learn it, but they kept forgetting, and so he had to spend all the afternoon and evening teaching them the Lord's Prayer. At last they thought they remembered it, so he got back on board the ship and continued his journey feeling he had done a good day's pastoral work.

But it was such a strange experience, meeting the three old men hand in hand on the shore, he could not go to sleep. He sat on deck thinking about the day. And what should he see? Following the boat moving rapidly across the water, a bright light! As it came closer, he realized it was the three old men, all illumined with light skimming across the waters, their white beards flying in the wind. They caught up with the boat and greeted the bishop, "Holy bishop, bless us!" And he bowed low, "And pray for me." Then the three old men said, "We have forgotten the prayer. Teach us again." And the bishop said, "Holy men, pray to God in your own way. Your prayer will reach Him." So they bowed low and skimmed across the waters back to their island. But long after they disappeared from view, there was still on the horizon a bright light.

I felt a bit like the three hermits earlier this evening when I couldn't remember the Dutch words for "Christ is risen!" That is why I told you that story. Only this time, it wasn't the holy men, but the bishop, who could not remember.

I want to continue with some reflections on the Liturgy. Last night I talked about the use of the word "peace" in the Divine Liturgy: "In peace let us pray to the Lord, for the peace from above, for the peace of the whole world." Then we reflected also on the meaning of the celebrant's greeting, "Peace be unto all." We saw how the priest is not just transmitting his own peace, but he is transmitting to them the peace of Christ. And peace, we said, is a gift from God.

Now, there is one phrase from the Liturgy in which the word peace figures prominently that I did not mention last night. I expected one of you in the discussion to say, "Why didn't you mention that?" But none of you did say that.

The phrase that I didn't mention last night that I want us to look at now is the one that comes after Holy Communion shortly before the final dismissal: "Let us go forth in peace."

There are many commandments in the Liturgy, many things that we are told to do such as "Lift up your hearts," "Give thanks to the Lord."

"Let us go forth in peace" is the last commandment of the Liturgy. What does it mean? It means, surely, that the conclusion of the Divine Liturgy is not an end but a beginning. Those words, "Let us go forth in peace," are not a comforting epilogue, they are a call to serve and bear witness. In effect, those words, "Let us go forth in peace," mean the Liturgy is over; the liturgy after the Liturgy is about to begin.

This, then, is the aim of the Liturgy: that we should return to the world with the doors of our perceptions cleansed. We should return to the world after the Liturgy, seeing Christ in every human person, especially in those who suffer. In the words of Father Alexander Schmemann, the Christian is the one who, wherever he or she looks, sees Christ everywhere and rejoices in Him. We are to go out, then, from the Liturgy and see Christ everywhere.

I was hungry. I was thirsty. I was a stranger. I was in prison (Mt 25.35–36). Of everyone who is in need, Christ says, "I." Christ is looking at us through the eyes of all the people whom we meet, and especially those who are in distress and who are suffering. So, we go out from the Liturgy, seeing Christ everywhere. But we are to return to the world not just with our eyes open but with our hands strengthened. There is a hymn I remember as an Anglican that we used to sing at the end of the Eucharist, "Strengthen for service, Lord, the hands that holy things have taken." It was said in the hymn book that this was from the Syrian liturgy. So, we are not only to see Christ in all human persons, but we are to serve Christ, to minister to Him, in all human persons.

Let us reflect on what happened at the Last Supper. First there was the eucharistic meal, where Christ blessed bread and gave it to the disciples: *This is my body*; and He blessed the cup: *This is my blood* (Mt 26.26, 28). Then, after the eucharistic meal, Christ kneels and washes the feet of His disciples. The eucharistic meal and the foot washing are a single mystery. So, we have to apply that to ourselves. We go out from the Liturgy to wash the feet of our fellow humans, literally and symbolically. That is how I understand the words at the end of the Liturgy, "Let us go forth in peace." Peace is to be something dynamic within this broken world. It is not merely a quality that we experience within the church walls.

Let us remind ourselves of the way in which Saint John Chrysostom envisages this liturgy after the Liturgy. There are, he says, two altars. There is, in the first place, the altar in church, and toward this altar we show deep reverence. We bow in front of it. We decorate it with silver and gold. We cover it with precious hangings. But, continues Saint John, there is another altar, an altar that we encounter every day, on which we can offer sacrifice at any moment. And yet toward this second altar, an altar that God Himself has made, we show no reverence at all. We treat it with contempt. We ignore it. And what is this second altar? It is, says Saint John Chrysostom, the poor, the suffering, those in need, the homeless, all who are in distress. At any moment, he says, when you go out from the church, there you will see an altar on which you can offer sacrifice, a living altar made by Christ.

Developing the meaning of the command, "Let us go forth in peace," let us think of the Liturgy as a journey. This is Father Alexander Schmemann's key image for the Liturgy. We may discern in the Liturgy a movement of ascent and of return. That kind of movement actually happens very frequently. We can see it in the lives of the saints— such saints as Antony of Egypt or Seraphim of Sarov. First, in the movement of ascent, if you like, or flight from the world, they go out into the desert, into the wilderness, into solitude, to be alone with God. But then there is a moment of return. They open their doors to the world, they receive all who come, they minister and they heal.

There is a similar movement of ascent within the Liturgy. We go to church. It is pleasant to walk there, though some people have to use cars. I like to walk from my home to church before the Divine Liturgy, to walk alone if I can. It is only about ten minutes for me, but it is quite important, I find, to have that movement, a sense of going to church, a sense, if you like, of a separation from the world and starting on a journey. I walk to church, I enter the church building, I enter within sacred space and sacred time. This is the beginning of the movement of ascent. We go to the church. Then, continuing the movement of ascent, we bring to the altar gifts of bread and wine, and we offer them to Christ. The movement of ascent is completed when Christ accepts this offering, consecrates it, makes the bread and wine to be His Body and His Blood.

After the ascent comes the return. The bread and wine that we offered to Christ, He then gives back to us in Holy Communion as His Body and Blood.

But the movement of return doesn't stop there. Having received Christ in the Holy Gifts, we then go out from the church, going back to the world to share Christ with all those around us.

Let us develop this idea a little. Receiving Christ's Body, we become what He is. We become the Body of Christ. But gifts are for sharing. So we become Christ's Body, not for ourselves, but for others. We become Christ's Body in the world and for the world. So the Eucharist impels believers to specific action in society, an action that will be challenging and prophetic. The Eucharist is the start of cosmic transfiguration, and each communicant shares in this transfiguring work.

Now this afternoon's talk has a very ambitious title—I cannot possibly deal with all the things suggested by it. That is the great danger—you think of the titles before you think of what you are actually going to say. So I just want now, in the light of what I have said about "Let us go forth in peace," to pose a few questions about the different levels of eucharistic healing and transfiguration in the world.

First, a question about our parish life. Perhaps this is not true of Vézelay, but it is true of some parishes that I have known elsewhere. I have often wondered why our parish council meetings, and more particularly the annual general meetings of parishes, are such a disappointment. To me it is very surprising that often there is a rather dark spirit at work in the annual general meetings of parishes. The picture given of our parish life is actually deeply misleading. All the good things seem to be hidden—perhaps that is as it should be—but we get a very distorted picture. There seems often to be an atmosphere of tension and hostility at annual general meetings in parishes.

I have often wondered why that is. How to bring a truly eucharistic spirit into such gatherings? How can we bring the peace of the Divine Liturgy into the other aspects of our parish life? I do not have an easy answer, but I think behind this first question there lurks another question. How can we make the Divine Liturgy more manifestly a shared and corporate action? In my own experience, the parish where I am, we began worshiping just in a room, and at that time it was not difficult to have a very strong feeling of the Liturgy as a unified action in which everybody was sharing because we were all so close to one another, and there were only a few of us.

Some of the most moving Liturgies I have ever attended have not been in churches with great marble floors and huge candelabra but in small house chapels in a room or even in a garage. Now, gradually our community has grown. Twenty-five years ago, we built ourselves a church, and now that church is too small, and we are working toward enlarging the church in order to be able to have room for all the worshipers. Now that is, in a sense, encouraging, but there is a real struggle here. As a parish grows larger, and as it acquires a larger building, it becomes much harder to preserve the corporate spirit, the sense of a single family, the sense of all of us doing something together. It becomes much harder to preserve that.

I have no easy answers here, but that is one level on which I ask: How can we bring peace and healing into a community that is growing larger all the time, and therefore that is bound to lose its sense of close coherence, unless we struggle to preserve it?

There is another level of healing that occurs to me quite frequently at the Divine Liturgy. We often have present non-Orthodox Christians, and we are not able to give them Holy Communion by the rules of our Church. Now, I am sure all of you have reflected on the reasons why the Orthodox Church takes this straight line over inter-communion. The act of Communion, we say, involves our total acceptance of the faith. It involves our total life in the Church. Therefore, we cannot share in Communion with other Christians who, however much we may love them, we recognize as holding a different understanding of the Christian faith, and who are divided from us.

This is, we know, the argument why we cannot have inter-communion. But I think we should constantly ask ourselves if we are right to take this position? In fact I think we are, but I would say go on asking yourself in your heart if it is the right thing to do. We Orthodox are becoming increasingly isolated on this issue. In my young days, most Anglicans would have taken the same view, and would have said they could not have communion with Protestants. That is certainly not the case now in the Anglican Church. Also, Roman Catholics held this view very strictly, but since Vatican II, whatever the official regulations may be, in the practice of the Roman Catholic Church there is widespread inter-communion. But we Orthodox continue as we were. Are we right? And if we do continue to uphold a strict line on inter-communion, in what spirit are we doing this? Is it in a spirit of peace and healing?

I remember at the beginning of my time as priest, the first occasion—and I still feel the wound inwardly—when persons came up for Communion whom I knew were not Orthodox. I felt that it was my duty as priest not to give them Communion. I was really interested in the reaction of two different parishioners. One said to me, "You did quite right! We cannot give Communion to these heretics. The Orthodox Church is the one true Church." He saw that in triumphalist terms. That made me feel even worse. But then another parishioner came up, and he said, in a very different tone of voice, "Yes, you were right, but how tragic, how sad, that we had to do this." Then I thought, yes, we do have to do this, but we should never do it in an aggressive spirit of superiority but always with a sense of deep sorrow in our hearts. We should mind very much that we cannot yet have Communion together. Incidentally, both of those two parishioners are now Orthodox priests themselves. I think the first one, over the years, has grown a little less triumphalist. I hope we all do, but I am not sure whether that always happens.

Then I would like to reflect on a third level of healing. Let me take as my basis here the words said just before the Epiclesis, the invocation of the Holy Spirit, at the heart of the Liturgy. The deacon lifts the Holy Gifts, and the celebrant says, "Thine own from Thine own, we offer Thee." And in usual translation, it continues, "on behalf of all and for all." But that translation could be misleading. It could be understood as meaning "for all human persons, for everyone." In fact in Greek, it is not masculine, it is neuter—"for in all things, and for all things." At that moment, we do not just speak about human persons, we speak about all created things. A more literal translation would be, "In all things and for all things."

This shows us that the liturgy after the Liturgy involves service not just for all persons, but ministry to the whole creation, to all created things. The Eucharist—that is to say—commits us to an ecological healing. That is underlined in the words I used from Father Lev last night: "Peace of the whole world." It means, says Father Lev, peace not just for humans, but all creatures—for animals and vegetables, stars, for all nature. Cosmic piety and cosmic healing. Ecology has become mildly fashionable now. It often has quite strong political associations. We Orthodox, along with other Christians, must involve ourselves fully in the movement on behalf of the environment, but we must do so in the name of the Divine Liturgy. We must put our ecological witness in the context of Holy Communion.

I am very much encouraged by the initiatives taken recently by the Ecumenical Patriarchate of Constantinople. Some ten years ago, the then Ecumenical Patriarch Dimitrios issued a Christmas encyclical saying that when we celebrate the incarnation of Christ, His taking of a human Body, we should also see that as God's blessing upon the whole creation. We should understand the incarnation in cosmic terms. He goes on in his encyclical to call all of us to show, and I quote, "toward the creation an ascetic and eucharistic spirit."[2] An ascetic spirit helps us distinguish between wants and needs.

The real question is not, "What do I want?" The real question is, "What do I need?" I want a great many things that I do not in fact need. The first step toward cosmic healing is for me to make a distinction between the two, and as far as possible, to stick to what I need. People want more and more. That is going to bring disaster on ourselves if we go on selfishly increasing our demands. But we do not in fact need more and more to be truly human. That is what I understand to define an ascetic spirit. Fasting indeed can help us to distinguish between what we want and what we need. Good to do without things, because then we realize that, yes, we can use them, but we can also forego them; we are not dependent on material things. We have freedom.

If we have a eucharistic spirit, we realize all is a gift to be offered back in thanksgiving to God the Giver. Developing this theme, the Ecumenical Patriarch Dimitrios, followed by his successor, the present Patriarch Bartholomew, have dedicated the first of September, the New Year in the Orthodox calendar, as a day of creation, when we give thanks to God for His gifts, when we ask forgiveness for the way we have misused those gifts, and when we pray that we may be guided for the right use of them in the future. There is a phrase that often comes to my mind from the special service "When in danger of earthquake." "The earth, though without words, yet cries aloud, 'Why, all peoples, do you inflict upon me such evil?'" And we are inflicting great evil on the earth. It is interesting to see earthquakes as the earth groaning because of what we do to it.

Finally, I ask you to think for a moment about this morning's Gospel. What happens when the risen Christ on

the first Easter Sunday appears to His disciples? Christ says
first to the disciples, *Peace be unto you* (Jn 20.19, 21). The first
thing that Christ speaks after rising from the dead is peace.
Then what does He do? He shows them His hands and His
side. Why does He do that? For recognition. Yes, to show
that here He is, the one whom they saw three days before
crucified, here He is, risen from the dead in the same Body
in which He suffered and died. But there is surely more to it
than that. What He is doing is showing that, though He is
risen from the dead, yet He still bears upon Him the marks
of His suffering. In the heart of the risen and glorified
Christ, there is still a place for our human suffering. When
Christ rises from the dead and ascends into heaven, He does
not disengage Himself from this broken world. On the contrary, He still carries on His Body the marks of His suffering, and He carries in His heart all our burdens. When He
says before His Ascension, *See I am with you, even to the end
of the world* (Mt 28.20), surely He means, "I am with you in
your distress and in your suffering." Glorified, He is still
with us. He has not rejected our suffering, nor disassociated
Himself from us.

We see from today's Gospel how peace goes with cross
bearing. Having given peace to His disciples, the risen

Christ immediately shows them the marks of the Cross. As I said in my first talk, peace means healing and wholeness, but we have to add: peace also means vulnerability. Peace, we might say, does not mean the absence of struggle or temptation or suffering. As long as we are in this world, we are to expect temptation and suffering. As Saint Antony of Egypt said, "Take away temptation and nobody will be saved."[3] So peace does not mean the absence of struggle, but peace means commitment, firmness of purpose, clarity of vision, an undivided heart, and a willingness to bear the burdens of others. When Paul says, *See, I bear in my body the marks, the stigmata, of Christ crucified* (Gal 6.17), he is describing his state of peace.

6

"A Peaceful Ending to Our Life"

Bodily Death as an Experience of Healing

Our theme during these days together has been to explore peace, understood in terms of healing, of wholeness. So we looked at the wholeness of the human person in my first two talks, and the third we began to speak of the sacraments, and of Confession as a sacrament of healing. My fourth and fifth talks were related to the Liturgy, the theme of peace of the Liturgy, and now, in the last of my addresses, let us look together at death, and let us ask how death can be an experience of healing. What is the connection between death and peace?

Now, if we take as our guide Orthodox prayers, we see that there is a connection. Often death and peace are mentioned together. Take for example from our evening prayers, the prayer divided into twenty-four short sections, that is attributed to Saint John Chrysostom. One of the short prayers runs: "O Lord, grant me tears, mindfulness of death, and a sense of peace." Surely, the context here is significant. Death is mentioned between "tears" and "a sense of peace." Now, in the Orthodox understanding of tears, they may indeed signify repentance for sin, but tears can also mean tears of joy at the love of God. We weep in our personal human relations when we suddenly discover that someone else loves us very much, and so we weep also when we recognize how much we are loved by Christ. So tears involve joy, and we notice how mindfulness of death is linked with the sense of peace as well as with tears. Death is not to be a subject of anxiety and fear. It is linked with wholeness and hope. "Grant me tears, mindfulness of death, and a sense of peace."

The same connection between death and peace comes in the petition from the litany used at the Divine Liturgy, and at Orthros, and at Vespers. We pray for "a Christian ending to our life, painless, blameless, peaceful, and a good defense before the dread judgement seat of Christ." So once more there is a connection here between death and peace.

We notice the same connection in a passage from Saint Isaac the Syrian, which could be taken as expressing in classic terms the Orthodox attitude to death. Prepare your heart for your departure, says Saint Isaac. If you are wise you will expect it every hour.

> Fix your departure in your heart, O man, by always saying to yourself: "Behold, the messenger is at the door, he who comes for me. Why am I idle? My going forth is forever; there will be no return." Pass the night in this reflection; muse upon this thought throughout the day. And when the time of departure comes, greet it with gladness, saying: "Come in peace! I knew that you were coming and I have not neglected anything that could prove useful to me on the way."[1]

Now what strikes me in that passage is a sense of sobriety and of gentle realism, and a sense of peacefulness. Prepare your heart for your departure. There is no way of avoiding death, unless the second coming happens in our lifetime—which it may, but that we do not know. But what strikes me particularly about Saint Isaac is that death for him is not something that we should think about with revulsion and horror but with quiet eagerness. "When the time for departure comes, go joyfully to meet him."

"Come in peace"—that is what we have to say to the angel of death when he appears to us. "I knew you would come, I knew I had to go on this journey, so I have got my little suitcase ready and we can set out now." That is the spirit in which we are to think about our coming death.

There are all kinds of preparations we can make, unless we are monastics living by strict poverty, which I am not. We should all of us make a will, as it causes great inconvenience to our friends and relatives if we don't make a will. We should sort out our papers and correspondence. My house is full of thousands of sheets of paper, and I dread to think what would happen if I died suddenly, which I may, so I ought to sort them out as otherwise I leave a difficult burden for other people. But there is something far more important that we should do to prepare for death, and that is mutual forgiveness. We should seek to be reconciled with all those from whom we are estranged. We should ask pardon and accept it, and we should take care not to leave this for the last moment, for we do not know when the last moment will come.

We live in a culture where it is bad taste to talk about death. Televisions, newspapers, and modern novels are filled with violence and death, but it is bad taste to make it personal, to say, "I shall die and so will you." President Mitterrand shortly before his death, when he knew he was going to die, made some very interesting statements. "How do we learn to die?" he asked. "We live in a world that panics at this question and turns away." And he said we must resist the modern deficient relationship with death in this hurried existence.[2] In fact, there is a conspiracy of silence about death, but the true Orthodox Christian approach is that we should be mindful of our death, exactly as Saint Isaac says.

Now tonight I would like to explore two aspects of death, understood in terms of personal healing. First, let us take note how death and birth go together, and let us note that in this context death is far closer to us than we commonly imagine. Before our great death, the end of our life, we pass through many other deaths, and in each stage in our life death goes with growth. So perhaps we should see death as the final stage in our growth as persons. That is my first theme.

My second theme is to ask: How should we regard death—as an enemy or as a friendly companion—or perhaps as both? Is our death to be seen as a tragedy, or as healing, or perhaps both?

First then, birth and death. Let me start with three quotations. My first is from T. S. Eliot, because the poets are often the best theologians. This is from his poem "The Dry Salvages" in *Four Quartets*: "The time of death is every moment."[3] My second quotation is from the Victorian author George MacDonald. In his letters he says, "Death is only the outward form of birth."[4] And finally, I have a phrase from the Anaphora of the Liturgy of Saint Basil to which we have been listening and praying during the Great Fast and Holy Week. In the Anaphora it says, concerning Christ, "When He was about to go forth to His voluntary, awesome, and life-giving death." Let us hold fast to that phrase "life-giving death."

Death is far closer than we imagine. "The time of death is every moment." It is not just a distant event at the conclusion of our earthly existence. It is a present reality going on all the time around us and within us. All living is a kind of dying; we are dying all the time. But in this daily experience of dying, each death is followed by a new birth. All dying is also a kind of living. Life and death are not opposites, mutually exclusive, but they are intertwined. Our whole existence is a mixture of mortality and resurrection—as Paul says, *Dying and behold, we live* (2 Cor 6.9). The whole of life is a constant passover, passing over through death into new life. We should never think of death alone; we should always think of death and resurrection.

Now let us think about our life cycle, and here I am drawing on a talk which impressed me very much when I read it some years ago by a Scottish Roman-Catholic priest. Whoever thought that your bed is a very dangerous place—because ninety-five percent of people die in their beds! And yet as I get older, I find going to bed and falling asleep is something that I look forward to. Falling asleep each night is in fact a foretaste of death but is not a frightening experience. Because this foretaste of death is followed each morning by a foretaste of resurrection. When we awake the next morning, it is as if the world has been created anew. I like the Hebrew benediction, "Blessed art Thou, O Lord our God, King of the universe, who createst Thy world every morning afresh."[5] So falling asleep at night, waking up the next morning, is in its way a passing over through death into new life. Might not our eventual death be like that? A falling asleep followed by an awakening. We are not afraid to drop off to sleep each night, because we feel confident we are going to wake up once more next morning. But perhaps we won't. Can we not with Christ's help feel something of the same trust about our final falling asleep in death? May we not expect to wake up again in eternity?

I remember talking with my own father before his death. He had been a regular soldier. He had fought in both World Wars. He had had a great deal of experience of being in danger of death—certainly he had seen a great deal of death around him in those two wars. He confided in me shortly before he died that he was afraid of death, and I said to him, "Well, may it not be like falling asleep?" And in fact that was exactly how it was in his case. He fell asleep and he died in his sleep. He knew he was likely to die quite soon, and he had made his preparations. Well, that is one example of the way death and resurrection are intertwined in our daily life.

Then let us think about growing up. Each time we pass from one stage of life into another, something dies in us so that something else can come alive. The transition—say, from being a child to becoming an adolescent—can often actually be quite painful and stormy. There is a death—the child has to die in us so that the growing adult may come alive. Perhaps there is another inner death when we pass from adolescence to being a mature adult.

These transitions are often painful and crisis-ridden. I read an account some time ago of Jesus at age twelve in the Temple. At first I was a little offended. Should we think of Christ in those terms? And then I thought, well, He was truly human; therefore, He was a real human child, and He went through all the processes of growth that we went through. The author was commenting on the incident of the twelve-year-old Jesus in the Temple and said—and I think that is true—that Mary and Joseph recognized they had a crisis on their hands when Jesus began to show independence as a teenager. This is one way of looking at it, and perhaps not such an irreverent way.

So all through our life, if we are to grow, we have got to be willing to let something die in us. If we refuse death, if we draw back from making the transition, we cannot become real persons. And here I would quote George Mac-Donald again, this time from his novel *Lilith*: "You will be dead so long as you refuse to die."[6] We have to yield things, to give them up, if we are to receive new gifts. But in growing up, each crisis of growth is also a lesson in love. Let me quote a poem by Cecil Day Lewis called "Walking away," where he is talking of leaving his young son for the first time at school.

It is eighteen years ago, almost to the day—
A sunny day with leaves just turning,
The touch-lines new-ruled—since I watched
     you play
Your first game of football, then, like a
     satellite
Wrenched from its orbit, go drifting away

Behind a scatter of boys. I can see
You walking away from me towards the
     school
With the pathos of a half-fledged thing set
     free
Into a wilderness, the gait of one
Who finds no path where the path should be.

That hesitant figure, eddying away
Like a winged seed loosened from its parent
     stem,
Has something I never quite grasp to convey
About nature's give-and-take—the small, the
     scorching
Ordeals which fire one's irresolute clay.

> I have had worse partings, but none that so
> Gnaws at my mind still. Perhaps it is roughly
> Saying what God alone could perfectly
>   show—
> How selfhood begins with a walking away,
> And love is proved in the letting go.[7]

Another form of death is of course parting from friends and places, yet such partings are a necessary element in our growth. Unless we have sometimes the courage to leave familiar surroundings, to part with existing friends, and to forge new links, we do not realize our potential as persons. By hanging on to the old, we refuse the invitation to discover the new. As Cecil Day Lewis said, "Selfhood begins with a walking away / And love is proved in the letting go." That is a lesson we have to learn and relearn throughout our lives.

Rejection is another form of death that we have to face, all of us, at some point in our lives. As you probably know, my work is to teach in university, and I have seen—particularly in the last ten years, with the unemployment in Britain—how very difficult it is even for those who get quite a good degree in university then to find a job. They have to write not ten but perhaps a hundred times, applying for jobs, before they find one. Each time you apply for a job you are offering yourself. Here am I with all my qualities—won't you find a place for me? Each time you get a letter saying no, you undergo a certain death, a very hard death, as you face that disappointment, and yet perhaps that is what we have to learn if we are to become real persons.

Another kind of rejection, of course, and more profound, is rejection in love—when we love someone else, and we find that our love is not returned. As children, if we come from happy homes, we often take love for granted. We assume that our parents will love and care for us. But then when we grow up, we find we cannot assume that from other people—they are free and they may feel, yes, we are nice enough people, but they do not love us in the way that we love them. Perhaps for many of us in our young years, the experience of being disappointed in love is the moment when we really begin to grow up, because bereavement is a form of death, not just for the one who dies but also for the one who remains alive. Yet bereavement faced inwardly and accepted through prayer, for that time is needed, makes us more authentically alive than we were before.

Another kind of death is the death of faith. Our Christian life surely has to be a journey, an exploration. We may at different times in our lives lose apparently our root certainties, or what we thought were certainties, about God and His existence. One symbolic interpretation of the Ten Commandments holds that, when it is said that you are to have no idols, that means also mental idols: conceptual and intellectual idols. All through our lives we have to be willing to shatter our idols about God, the ideas that we had, in order to come closer to the living God. To be fully alive, our faith must repeatedly die.

Of course, long before we actually die, growing old is an experience of death. As we get older, we have to be willing to yield the central place in the limelight to others, to let them shine. We have to apply to ourselves to what John the Baptist says, *He must increase and I must decrease* (Jn 3.30). As a teacher I think sometimes of the Jewish saying: "Blessed is the teacher who has pupils who are cleverer than he." Teachers do not usually like it that pupils are cleverer, but that is something we have to accept, especially as we get older, that they are going to be more brilliant, more up-to-date, and more fashionable than we are.

Surely the secret of true life is to accept each state as it comes. To die the death and to live the new life, not to cling to the past but to live with total integrity in the present. Now in all these cases out of dying there comes resurrection. Not loss but enrichment, not decay but growth. To say that something dies means that something comes alive. May not the death that comes right at the end of our life fit into that pattern? May not our bodily death be the final stage in our growth, the last and greatest in the long series of deaths and resurrections, which we have been experiencing ever since the day we were born? If the small deaths each lead beyond death to resurrection, may this not be true of the great death that awaits us when we finally leave this world? May this not be the greatest passover? Then we should enlarge our vision, we should look beyond our own life stories to the Christ story. We should relate the death and resurrection pattern within our own life to the Death and Resurrection of Jesus our Savior that we have just been celebrating. Our story makes sense in the light of His story. Our small deaths and resurrections are joined across history through His definitive Death and Resurrection. What did we hear at Paschal midnight? "Let none fear death, for the death of the Savior has set us free. He has destroyed death by undergoing death. Christ is risen and death reigns in fear. Christ is risen and there is none dead in the tomb."[8]

Now, when people change their tapes over, I know that means I have been talking quite a long time, so I will try and speed things up. That was my first theme. In Eliot's words, "A time of death is every moment," that death is not closer than we think, but death goes with growth and resurrection.

Now I want to look at the second question: "Is death an enemy or friendly companion?" My answer here is that our attitude toward death should not be blind terror but awe and wonder.

What is death? Let me offer you two definitions. The first is from Clement of Alexandria, in the early third century. "Death," he says, "is the separation from the soul and the body."[9] My second definition is from Saint Maximus the Confessor, who writes, "Death in the true sense is the separation from God."[10] Now I think both definitions are true, but the second comes closer to the heart of the matter. Clement speaks of physical death, the separation of soul and body—the heart stops beating, the breathing ceases, the body grows cold and later dissolves. But Saint Maximus goes further. He speaks about spiritual death. Death, in the deep sense, is the separation of the total person, soul and body together from God. Life is communion with God;

losing that communion we die. Now the corollary of this is that many people die before their deaths. Outwardly and physically they are still alive, but inwardly and spiritually they are already dead. Their souls have died before their bodies. Animated corpses walk about in our midst, and we meet them every day.

Now spiritual death, as separation from God, means a state of sinfulness. In Scripture death and sin are very closely related. Death is an aspect of our fallen condition. In the Genesis story, disobedience to God's command brings death. God says, *On the day you eat from the tree which you are told not to eat from, you shall surely die* (Gen 2.17). So the real death is not physical but spiritual.

Now is death an enemy or a friend? From one point of view, it is an enemy. The true person, of the Christian understanding as I have already said in my opening talk, is an undivided unity of soul and body together. The body is not a prison or tomb.[11] It is an integral part of our personhood. As C. G. Jung says, "Spirit is the living body seen from within and the body the outer manifestation of the living spirit."[12] So death from this point of view is not natural. It is profoundly unnatural. It is an affront against the wholeness of our human nature. It is not what God intended for us. He did not create us for death but for life. Death in this sense is monstrous and tragic. It is, in Paul's words, *an enemy to be destroyed* (1 Cor 15.26), and hence Christ's grief and tears at the grave of His friend Lazarus. *Jesus wept* (Jn 11.35). If He wept at the face of death, so may we. Saint Paul tells us not to refrain altogether from sorrow, but he simply says we are not to sorrow as others do who have no hope (1 Thess 4.13). So he does not disapprove of all sorrow, only unbelieving, hopeless sorrow. I often think of that beautiful passage in *The Brothers Karamazov*, where Staretz Zosima speaks with a woman who has lost her child, and he does not tell her stop weeping; he tells her that she should weep. And yet he says the time will come when, through your weeping, you will reach peace.[13] Tears can have a healing effect; the bereaved need to be allowed to mourn, and they have to have time for their mourning.

What I find impressive about the Orthodox funeral service is that people do not feel ashamed to weep. I was brought up in a culture that thought a funeral should be very tight lipped and restrained, dignified. If people broke down and showed grief, the others were embarrassed. But thank God, in the Orthodox Church, we are not embarrassed.

If Christ wept, so may we. At Gethsemane, Christ felt real anguish in the face of death. He did feel a sense of horror at His own coming death. So death can be seen as an enemy, but it is also a friend. It may be monstrous, but it can be full of beauty. Yes, we do feel grief at the death of those we love, but the sorrow can be a sorrow that leads to joy. Death is not part of God's original purpose for us but is in a fallen world part of His loving providence. There is a Russian fable that Jim [Forest] probably knows better than I do. Once upon a time a peasant was walking in the woods and he met death. Being quite an alert character, very quickly he put his sack over death's head and tied him up inside the sack and took him back home all tied up. Death struggled and shouted, but the person said, "I am not going to let you out." At first everybody said he was a marvelous man because he got rid of death. But then people just went on living. They got older and older, and their rheumatism got worse and worse. They grew more and more tired, but there was no release. They just had to go on living. So after a time they came to the man and said, "For goodness sake, let death out again, so we can have a way of escape." I think that is true in the fallen world: simply to live forever in this fallen world is not endurable. God in His mercy has given us a way of escape.

That is the way Jeremiah sees it when he uses the analogy of the potter. He goes down, in Jeremiah chapter 18, to the potter's house, and he sees how the pot has been spoiled on the wheel. The potter then shatters the clay and reworks it. So death is the shattering of the pot, so that it may be refashioned.[14] It is also what we say in the funeral service: "Of old Thou hast created me from nothing and honored me with Thy divine image, but when I disobeyed Thy commandment, Thou hast returned me to the earth whence I was taken. Lead me back again to Thy likeness, refashioning my ancient beauty."[15] So there death is seen as a way in which we are led back again to our true home, we are refashioned. So death is also a friend.

Just before supper I went into the basilica and went round to the place where there is a statue of Francis of Assisi. The Canticle of the Sun is posted there. I read Francis' words written just before his death: "Praised be my Lord for our sister, bodily death."[16] Death is the means of our return to God. It is an encounter with Christ. It could be transformed into an act of worship, into an experience of healing. It is a friend, not an enemy. It is a beginning, not an end.

I think of the last words of the Russian thinker Prince Trubetskoy. As he was dying, he said, "The royal doors are open, the great Liturgy is about to begin."[17]

Abbreviations

ANF   *The Ante-Nicene Fathers. Translations of the Writings of the Fathers Down to A.D. 325.* 10 volumes. Edited by Alexander Roberts and James Donaldson. Buffalo, NY: The Christian Literature Company, 1885–1896, and many reprints.

NPNF[1]   *A Select Library of Nicene and Post-Nicene Fathers of the Christian Church.* First Series. 14 volumes. Edited by Philip Schaff. Buffalo, NY: The Christian Literature Company, 1886–1900, and many reprints.

NPNF[2]   *A Select Library of Nicene and Post-Nicene Fathers of the Christian Church.* Second Series. New York: The Christian Literature Company, 1886–1900, and many reprints.

PG   *Patrologiae Cursus Completus: Series Graeca.* 161 volumes. Edited by J.-P. Migne. Paris, 1857–1866.

Philokalia *The Philokalia: The Complete Text*. 5 volumes. Compiled by Saint Nikodimos of the Holy Mountain and Saint Makarios of Corinth. Translated by G. E. H. Palmer, Philip Sherrard, and Kallistos Ware. London: Faber and Faber, 1979–2023.

PPS   Popular Patristics Series. Crestwood/Yonkers, NY: St Vladimir's Seminary Press, 1996–

Endnotes

Metropolitan Kallistos was well-known for his "easy reference to quotations," as Father Andrew Louth puts it in the foreword to this book. But since few possess the breadth and depth of his learning, the following notes provide citations, information on English translations, and some brief elucidations to help those who want to read and understand more about the many Church Fathers, thinkers, and poets who are quoted here. At times Met. Kallistos paraphrased sources or provided his own translation. Usually, his words were kept as they were delivered, but at times they were changed to make it easier to consult published translations.

—*Editor*

1

"Glorify God with Your Body"

1 St Nicholas Cabasilas, *The Life in Christ* 1.6; English translation: Nicholas Cabasilas, *The Life in Christ*, trans. Carmino J. deCatanzaro (Crestwood, NY: St Vladimir's Seminary Press, 1998), 49–50.

2 Ibid.

3 The Kosovo War took place from February 28, 1998, to June 11, 1999. NATO conducted bombing campaigns (including bombings on Pascha itself, as Met. Kallistos mentions) in which many Serbian Orthodox Christians lost their homes and their lives.

4 Elsewhere, Met. Kallistos provided this citation: Ivan Kologrivof, *Essai sur la sainteté en Russie* (Bruges: Beyaert, 1953), 430. It can also be found in English in these more readily available books: Valentine Zander, *St Seraphim of Sarov*, trans. Sister Gabriel Anne, S.S.C. (Crestwood, NY: St Vladimir's Seminary Press, 1975), x; Archimandrite Lazarus (Moore), *An Extraordinary Peace: St. Seraphim, Flame of Sarov* (Port Townsend, WA: Anaphora Press, 2009), 30.

5 The Renaissance thinker Giovanni Pico della Mirandola delivered his *Oration on the Dignity of Man* in 1486, and it was first published in 1496. He attributes the phrase "the marriage song of the world" to Persian sages at the very beginning of the *Oration*; English translation: Giovanni Pico della Mirandola, *Oration on the Dignity of Man*, trans.

A. Robert Caponigri (Chicago: Henry Regnery Company, 1956), 4.

6 Origen, *Homilies on Leviticus* 5.3; English translation: *Origen: Homilies on Leviticus 1–16*, trans. Gary Wayne Barkely, Fathers of the Church 83 (Washington, DC: The Catholic University of America, 1990), 92.

7 In this section, Met. Kallistos draws especially upon *Oration* 38.10–11: "And since the first world was beautiful to God, he thought a second material and visible world, that which is composed of heaven and earth and the system and composite of realities existing between them. . . . [T]he Creator Word also makes one living creature out of both, I mean invisible and visible natures, that is the human being. And having taken the body from the matter already created, he breathed in breath from himself, which is surely the intelligent soul and the image of God of which Scripture speaks. The human being is a kind of second world, great in smallness, placed on the earth, another angel, a composite worshiper, a beholder of the visible creation, an initiate into the intelligible, king of things on earth, subject to what is above, earthly and heavenly, transitory and immortal, visible and intelligible, a mean between greatness and lowliness. He is at once spirit and flesh, spirit on account of grace, flesh on account of pride, the one that he might remain and glorify his Benefactor, the other that he might suffer and in suffering remember and be corrected if he has ambition for

greatness." St Gregory of Nazianzus, *Festal Orations*, trans. Nonna Verna Harrison, Popular Patristics Series 36 (Crestwood, NY: St Vladimir's Seminary Press, 2008), 67–68.

8 This is a central theme in St Maximus, explored at length in Lars Thunberg, *Microcosm and Mediator: Theological Anthropology of Maximus the Confessor*, 2nd ed. (Chicago: Open Court Publishing Company, 1995)—a simpler version can be found in Lars Thunberg, *Man and the Cosmos: The Vision of St Maximus the Confessor* (Crestwood, NY: St Vladimir's Seminary Press, 2012). This theme is beautifully exemplified in St Maximus' *Ambiguum* 41, to which Met. Kallistos alludes below (see n. 10).

9 St Gregory of Nyssa, *On the Making of Man* 16.1 (NPNF[2] 5:404).

10 St Maximus the Confessor, *Ambiguum* 41 (esp. PG 91:1304D–1312B); English translation: Maximos the Confessor, *On Difficulties in the Fathers*, vol. 2, ed. and trans. Nicholas Constas, Dumbarton Oaks Medieval Library 29 (Cambridge, MA: Harvard University Press, 2014), 103–115.

11 For some of Berdyaev's arguments regarding the concept of *microtheos*, see Nicholas Berdyaev, *The Beginning and the End*, trans. R. M. French (New York: Harper & Bros., 1952), 3–88.

12 St Basil, *First Homily on Fasting* 10; English translation: St Basil the Great, *On Fasting and Feasts*, trans. Susan R.

Holman and Mark DelCogliano, Popular Patristics Series
50 (Yonkers, NY: St Vladimir's Seminary Press, 2013), 69.

13 From Larkin's poem "Water," in Philip Larkin, *The Whitsun Weddings* (London: Faber & Faber, 1964), 20.

14 In the Greek tradition, the mystery of Holy Unction is served for the entire parish community (all of whom are anointed) on Great and Holy Wednesday in Holy Week. It is also, of course, served for individuals in cases of grave illness and for one who is about to die. For more on the history and theology of the Unction Service, as well as its text, see Paul Meyendorff, *The Anointing of the Sick*, The Orthodox Liturgy 1 (Crestwood, NY: St Vladimir's Seminary Press, 2009).

15 (Ps.-)Dionysius the Areopagite, *Ecclesiastical Hierarchy* 7.1.3; English translation: Dionysius the Areopagite, *The Celestial Hierarchy, the Ecclesiastical Hierarchy, and the Letters*, trans. Rev. Silviu Bunta and Abp Alexander Golitzin, Popular Patristics Series [no. TBA] (Yonkers, NY: St Vladimir's Seminary Press, forthcoming).

16 St Maximus the Confessor, *Two Hundred Chapters on Theology* 2.88; English translation: *Two Hundred Chapters on Theology*, trans. Luis Joshua Salés, Popular Patristics Series 53 (Yonkers, NY: St Vladimir's Seminary Press, 2015), 171. Palamas cites this approvingly in *Triads* 1.3.37.

17 St Gregory Palamas, *Triads* 1.2.9; English translation: St Gregory Palamas, *Triads*, trans. Alexander Titus, Popular

Patristics Series 5 (Yonkers, NY: St Vladimir's Seminary
Press, forthcoming).

18 St Gregory Palamas, *The Declaration of the Holy Mountain
in Defense of Those Who Devoutly Practice a Life of Stillness*
(=*Hagiorite Tome*) 6; English translation: *Philokalia* 4:423.

19 Porphyry, *Life of Plotinus* 1, 2; English translation: *Plotinus,
Volume 1: Pophryry On Plotinus, Ennead 1*, rev. ed., trans.
A. H. Armstrong, Loeb Classical Library 440 (Cambridge,
MA: Harvard University Press, 1969), 3, 7.

20 William Blake, *The Marriage of Heaven and Hell* (Oxford:
Oxford University Press, 1975), xvi.

21 Sophocles, *Antigone*, line 332; English translation (by Elizabeth Wyckoff): *Sophocles I*, The Complete Greek Tragedies
(The University of Chicago Press, 1954), 170.

22 The notion that the human person is incomprehensible
emerged with special clarity in the Eunomian controversy.
The radical Arian Eunomius claimed that the Son was
not "consubstantial," or of the same substance, with the
Father but rather of an unlike substance (hence the title
"Anomoean," from the Greek word *anomoios*, "unlike").
Eunomius held that the substance or essence of God the
Father was unbegottenness, making the Only-Begotten
Son by definition of a different substance. The Cappadocian
Fathers ridiculed the notion that God's essence could be
known. They rebutted this by stating that even the essence
of man is unknown and unknowable, let alone the divine.

See, for example, St Gregory of Nyssa, *Against Eunomius* 2.117, 3.4.

2
The Passions: Enemy or Friend?

1 For an Orthodox engagement with these texts, see Edith M. Humphrey, *Further Up and Further In: Orthodox Conversations with C. S. Lewis on Scripture and Theology* (Yonkers, NY: St Vladimir's Seminary Press, 2017).

2 Plato, *Theaetetus* 155d; English translation (by M. J. Levitt, rev. Myles Burnyeat): *Plato: Complete Works*, ed. John M. Cooper (Indianapolis, IN: Hackett Publishing Company, 1997), 173.

3 St Isaac the Syrian, *Ascetical Homilies*, Homily 2; English translation: *The Ascetical Homilies of Saint Isaac the Syrian* (Brookline, MA: Holy Transfiguration Monastery, 2011), 121.

4 Pascal, *Pensées* 277; English translation: *Pascal's Pensées*, trans. W. F. Trotter (New York: E. P. Dutton & Co., 1958), 78. Wallis Simpson's memoir, *The Heart Has Its Reasons: The Memoirs of the Duchess of Windsor* (London: Michael Joseph, 1956) evoked a different and more emotional interpretation of Pascal. King Edward VIII famously abdicated the throne of Great Britain to marry her in 1937.

5 St Macarius, *Spiritual Homilies* 15.20; English translation: *Fifty Spiritual Homilies of St Macarius the Egyptian*, trans.

A. J. Mason (London: Society for Promoting Christian Knowledge, 1921), 116.

6 St Macarius, *Spiritual Homilies* 15.32 (trans. Mason, 122).

7 Antoine de Saint-Exupéry, *The Little Prince*, trans. Katherine Woods (Thorndike, ME: G. K. Hall, 1995 [1st ed. 1943]), 139 (Chapter 21).

8 St Palladius, *Lausiac History* 2.2; English translation: *The Lausiac History of Palladius*, trans. W. K. Lowther Clarke (London: Society for Promoting Christian Knowledge, 1918), 49.

9 *Alphabetical Sayings of the Desert Fathers*, Abba Poemen 183; English translation: *Give Me a Word: The Alphabetical Sayings of the Desert Fathers*, trans. John Wortley, Popular Patristics Series 52 (Yonkers, NY: St Vladimir's Seminary Press, 2014), 258.

10 John Donne (1572–1631) was one of the "metaphysical poets," a group of seventeenth-century English poets who explored religious and philosophical themes, using surprising and inventive conceits (or images), together with colloquial diction and unusual or flexible meter. The quotation is from "The Litanie," a prayer in verse (Stanza 27, line 8—line 242 in the poem as a whole); John Donne, *The Complete English Poems of John Donne*, ed. C. A. Patrides (London: J. M. Dent & Sons, 1985), 467. This phrase is well-known to many modern readers as the epigraph to C. S. Lewis, *The Four Loves* (London: HarperCollins, 1960).

11 Sir Roger L'Estrange was an English writer and courtier, a
    staunch royalist and a loyal supporter of King Charles II in
    the Restoration era. This quotation comes from his version
    of Aesop's fables: Sir Roger L'Estrange, *Fables of Aesop and
    Other Eminent Mythologists: With Morals and Reflexions*,
    3rd rev. ed. (London: Printed for R. Sare, T. Sawbridge, B.
    Took, M. Gillyflower, A. & I. Churchil, and I. Hindmarsh,
    1669), 38. This occurs in his reflection upon the fable of the
    horse and the ass.

12 Stoics frequently use both *apatheia* and *ataraxia* to describe
    this state: "If you intend to improve, throw away such
    thoughts as these: if I neglect my affairs, I shall not have the
    means of living: unless I chastise my slave, he will be bad.
    For it is better to die of hunger and so to be released from
    grief and fear than to live in abundance with perturbation;
    and it is better for your slave to be bad than for you to be
    unhappy. Begin then from little things. Is the oil spilled? Is
    a little wine stolen? Say on the occasion, at such price is sold
    freedom from perturbation [*apatheia*]; at such price is sold
    tranquility [*ataraxia*], but nothing is got for nothing." Epic-
    tetus, *Discourses* 1.12; English translation: *The Discourses
    of Epictetus, with the Encheiridion and Fragments*, trans.
    George Long (London: George Bell and Sons, 1890), 383.
    The negative assessment of *pathos* can be seen, for instance,
    in the Roman Stoic Cicero, when he seeks to render the
    word in Latin: ". . . the emotions of the mind . . . harass and

embitter the life of the foolish (the Greek term for these is *pathos*, and I might have rendered this literally, styled them 'diseases' [*morbos*], but the word 'disease' would not suit all instances; for example, no one speaks of pity, nor yet anger, as a disease, though the Greeks term these *pathos*. Let us then accept the word 'emotion' [*perturbatio*] the very sound of which seems to denote something vicious, and these emotions are not excited by any natural influence." *De Finibus Bonorum et Malorum* 3.35; English translation: *De Finibus Bonorum et Malorum*, trans. H. Rackham, Loeb Classical Library 40 (Cambridge, MA: Harvard University Press, 1931), 255.

13 Aristotle lists fourteen kinds of *pathos* in his *Rhetoric*: anger, calm, friendship, enmity, fear, confidence, shame, shamelessness, kindness, unkindness, pity, indignation, envy, and emulation (see *Rhetoric* 2.1–11; 1378a–1388b). Aristotle's conception of *pathos* is broad, varied, and nuanced: some of the *pathē* are good and others bad, while some are neutral.

14 E.g., Plato, *Phaedrus* 246a ff. (*Plato: Complete Works*, 524 ff.).

15 Clement of Alexandria continually describes the healing of passions in the spiritual life and cites the pre-Socratic philosopher Democritus when classifying *pathos* as a disease of the soul: "Our Instructor, the Word, therefore cures the unnatural passions of the soul by means of exhortations. . . . For while the 'physician's art,' according to

Democritus, 'heals the diseases of the body; wisdom frees the soul from passion.' But the good Instructor, the Wisdom, the Word of the Father, who made man, cares for the whole nature of His creature; the all-sufficient Physician of humanity, the Saviour, heals both body and soul." *Paedagogus* 1.2 (ANF 2:210).

16 To see how closely Evagrius associates the demons with the passions, we could take this programmatic statement and replace the word "demon" with "passion" without changing the meaning: "Of the demons opposing us in the practice of the ascetic life, there are three groups who fight in the front line: those entrusted with the appetites of gluttony, those who suggest avaricious thoughts, and those who incite us to seek the esteem of men. All the other demons follow behind and in their turn attack those already wounded by the first three groups. For one does not fall into the power of the demon of unchastity, unless one has first fallen because of gluttony: nor is one's anger aroused unless one is fighting for food or material possessions or the esteem of men. And one does not escape the demon of dejection, unless one no longer experiences suffering when deprived of these things. Nor will one escape pride, the first offspring of the devil, unless one has banished avarice, the root of all evil, since poverty makes a man humble, according to Solomon (cf. Prov. 10:4. LXX). In short, no one can fall into the power of any demon, unless he has been wounded by those of the

front line." *Texts on Discrimination in Respect of Passions and Thoughts* 1; English translation: *Philokalia*, 1:38.

17 See St Gregory of Nyssa, *On the Making of Man* 18.1–2: "For I think that from this beginning all our passions issue as from a spring, and pour their flood over man's life; and an evidence of my words is the kinship of passions which appears alike in ourselves and in the brutes; for it is not allowable to ascribe the first beginnings of our constitutional liability to passion to that human nature which was fashioned in the Divine likeness; but as brute life first entered into the world, and man, for the reason already mentioned, took something of their nature (I mean the mode of generation), he accordingly took at the same time a share of the other attributes contemplated in that nature; for the likeness of man to God is not found in anger, nor is pleasure a mark of the superior nature; cowardice also, and boldness, and the desire of gain, and the dislike of loss, and all the like, are far removed from that stamp which indicates Divinity. These attributes, then, human nature took to itself from the side of the brutes; for those qualities with which brute life was armed for self-preservation, when transferred to human life, became passions; for the carnivorous animals are preserved by their anger, and those which breed largely by their love of pleasure; cowardice preserves the weak, fear that which is easily taken by more powerful animals, and greediness those of great

bulk; and to miss anything that tends to pleasure is for the brutes a matter of pain. All these and the like affections entered man's composition by reason of the animal mode of generation" (NPNF² 5:407–408). For more, see the entry "Apátheia" and the subsection "Passions and the Virtues" in the entry "Desire" in *The Brill Dictionary of Gregory of Nyssa*, ed. Lucas Francisco Mateo-Seco and Giulio Maspero, trans. Seth Cherney, Supplements to Vigiliae Christianae 99 (Leiden/Boston: Brill, 2010), 51–54, 220–21.

18 Abba Isaiah, Discourse 2; English translation: Abba Isaiah of Scetis, *Ascetic Discourses*, trans. John Chryssavgis and Pachomios (Robert) Penkett, Cistercian Studies Series 150 (Kalamazoo, MI: Cistercian Press, 2002), 44. For more of Met. Kallistos' thoughts on *pathos* in Abba Isaiah, see Kallistos Ware, "The Meaning of 'Pathos' in Abba Isaias and Theodoret of Cyrus," in *Studia Patristica* 20, ed. Elizabeth A. Livingstone (Leuven: Peeters, 1989), 315–22.

19 John Climacus, *Ladder* 26: "Physical love can be a paradigm of the longing for God. . . . Lucky the man who loves and longs for God as a smitten lover does for his beloved. . . . Someone truly in love keeps before his mind's eye the face of the beloved and embraces it there tenderly. Even during sleep the longing continues unappeased and he murmurs to his beloved. That is how it is for the body. And that is how it is for the spirit." (PG 88:1024B; 1156C–D); English translation: John Climacus, *The Ladder of Divine Ascent*, trans.

Colm Luibheid and Norman Russell, Classics of Western
Spirituality (Mahwah, NJ: Paulist Press, 1982), 287. For a
lengthier investigation of this positive sense of *eros* in the
Ladder, see Met. Kallistos' introduction to Russell's translation (esp. 31–33).

20 Abba Isaiah, Discourse 2 (trans. Chryssavgis and Penkett,
44).

21 Ibid. (modified).

22 Ibid. (modified).

23 Ibid.

24 Ibid.

25 Ibid.

26 Ibid.

27 Ibid., 44–45.

28 St Augustine's views on self-love were complex, but they
included a positive sense: "'The primal destruction of man
was self-love.' 'There is no one who does not love himself; but one must search for the right love and avoid the
warped.' 'Indeed you did not love yourself when you did
not love the God who made you.' These three sentences set
side by side show why the problem of self-love in St Augustine of Hippo constitutes a problem. Self-love is loving
God; it is also hating God. Self-love is common to all men;
it is restricted to those who love God. Mutually incom-
patible assertions about self-love jostle one another and
demand to be reconciled." Oliver O'Donovan, *The Problem*

of *Self-Love in St Augustine* (New Haven: Yale University Press, 1980), 1.

29 St Gregory Palamas, *Triads* 2.2.12; English translation: PPS 5 (forthcoming).

3
Approaching Christ the Physician
The True Meaning of Confession and Anointing

1 See Tito Colliander, *Way of the Ascetics: The Ancient Tradition of Discipline and Inner Growth*, trans. Katharine Ferré (Crestwood, NY: St Vladimir's Seminary Press, 1960), 54.

2 St Gregory of Nyssa, Canon 4 (from his Canonical Letter, i.e., Letter 31 to Letoius, Bishop of Melitene), approved by Canon 2 of the Council in Trullo; English translation: NPNF[2] 14:611; for a more recent translation of the entire Canonical Letter, see *Gregory of Nyssa: The Letters— Introduction, Translation and Commentary*, trans. Anna M. Silvas, Supplements to Vigiliae Christianae 83 (Leiden/ Boston: Brill, 2007), 221 (section 4.i).

3 St Basil the Great, Canon 59 (from his Third Canonical Letter, i.e., Letter 217 to Amphilochius of Iconium), approved by Canon 2 of the Council in Trullo; English translation: NPNF[2] 14:608; for the full letter see NPNF[2] 8:256.

4 St John the Faster, Canon 12; English translation: St Nikodemos the Hagiorite, *Exomologetarion: A Manual of*

Confession, trans. George Dokos (Thessalonica: Uncut Mountain Press, 2006), 234.

5 St John the Faster, Canon 24; *Exomologetarion*, 247.

6 See Fyodor Dostoevsky, *The Brothers Karamazov*, trans. Richard Pevear and Larissa Volokhonsky, Everyman's Library 70 (New York: Alfred A. Knopf, 1992), 25–59, 283–324 (for ease of reference to other translations and editions, references will also be given to Dostoevsky's divisions of parts, books, and chapters: 1.1.5–1.2.4, 2.6.1–3).

7 St John Chrysostom, *Homilies on John*, Homily 86.4 (NPNF[1] 14:326).

8 Dietrich Bonhoeffer, *Life Together* (New York: Harper and Row, 1954), 118. Bonhoeffer (1906–1945) was a German Lutheran pastor, theologian, and political dissident who opposed the Third Reich, which led to his arrest and, ultimately, to his execution on April 9, 1945.

4

"In Peace Let Us Pray to the Lord"

Peace and Healing in the Divine Liturgy

1 "In the perpetual miracle of the transubstantiation of the bread and wine into the true Body and Blood of Christ united with His Divinity and soul, I see the miracle of the perpetual quickening of man by the divine breathing, and of his creation into a living soul." John Iliytch Sergieff, *My*

Life in Christ, trans. E. E. Goulaeff (London, Paris & Melbourne: Cassell and Company Ltd, 1897), 114.

2 Cabasilas, *Life in Christ* 4.1 (trans. deCatanzaro, 114).

3 Dostoevsky, *Brothers Karamazov*, 352 (3.7.3: "An Onion").

4 Chrysostom, *Homilies on 2 Corinthians*, Homily 18.3 (NPNF[1] 12:366; commenting on 2 Cor 8.24).

5 A Monk of the Eastern Church [Lev Gillet], *Serve the Lord with Gladness: Basic Reflections on the Eucharist and the Priesthood*, trans. John Breck (Crestwood, NY: St Vladimir's Seminary Press, 1990).

6 "Ecstatic" comes from the Greek word *ekstasis*, which literally means to be beside or outside oneself.

7 Gillet, *Serve the Lord with Gladness*, 16.

8 Alexandre Semenoff-Tian-Chansky, *Father John of Kronstadt: A Life* (Crestwood, NY: St Vladimir's Seminary Press, 1979), 35.

5
"Let Us Go Forth in Peace"

Healing in the Parish, Local Church, and in the World

1 Leo Tolstoy wrote "The Three Hermits" (*Tri Startsa*) in 1885 and published it in 1886. It first appeared in English in Leo Tolstoy, *Twenty-Three Tales*, trans. Louise and Aylmer Maude (New York: Funk and Wagnalls Company, 1907); it has been republished many times.

2 Ecumenical Patriarch Dimitrios, Encyclical Letter on the
   Day of Protection of the Environment (September 1, 1989):
   "Unfortunately, in our days under the influence of an
   extreme rationalism and self-centeredness, man has lost
   the sense of the sacredness of creation and acts as its arbi-
   trary ruler and rude violator. Instead of the eucharistic and
   ascetic spirit with which the Orthodox Church brought up
   her children for centuries, we observe today a violation of
   nature for the satisfaction not of basic human needs, but
   of man's endless and constantly increasing desires of lust,
   encouraged by the prevailing philosophy of the consumer
   society." Ecumenical Patriarch Bartholomew, *On Earth as
   in Heaven: Ecological Vision and Initiatives of Ecumenical
   Patriarch Bartholomew*, ed. John Chryssavgis (New York:
   Fordham University Press, 2012), 24–25.
3 St Anthony the Great, *Alphabetical Sayings*, Anthony 5
   (PPS 52:32).

6

"A Peaceful Ending to Our Life"

Bodily Death as an Experience of Healing

1 St Isaac the Syrian, Homily 64; *Ascetical Homilies*, 459.
2 François Mitterrand was the president of France from 1981
   to 1995. As he was dying, he wrote the foreword to a book on
   death: Marie de Hennezel, *Intimate Death: How the Dying*

Teach us to Live, trans. Carol Brown Janeway (London: Little, Brown and Company, 1997), vii–x. In it, he wrote: "How do we learn to die? We live in a world that panics at this question and turns away. Other civilizations before ours looked squarely at death. They mapped the passage for both the community and the individual. They infused the fulfillment of destiny with a richness of meaning. Never perhaps have our relations with death been as barren as they are in this modern spiritual desert, in which our rush to a mere existence carries us past all sense of mystery. We do not even know that we are parching the essence of life of one of its wellsprings. . . . At the moment of utter solitude, when the body breaks down on the edge of infinity, a separate time begins to run that cannot be measured in any normal way. In the course of several days sometimes, with the help of another presence that allows despair and pain to declare themselves, the dying seize hold of their lives, take possession of them, unlock their truth. . . . Death can cause a human being to become what he or she was called to become; it can be, in the fullest sense of the word, an *accomplishment*." *Intimate Death*, vii, ix.

3 T. S. Eliot, *Four Quartets*, Part 3: "The Dry Salvages," Stanza 3, line 36.

4 George MacDonald, "Letters to Family" (1885); Gen. MSS 103:3.155. Quoted in Greville MacDonald, *George MacDonald and His Wife* (London: George Allen & Unwin Ltd, 1924), 248.

5   Barbara Green and Victor Gollancz, *God of a Hundred Names* (London: Gollancz, 1962), 19.

6   George MacDonald, *Lilith: A Romance* (New York: Dodd, Mead and Company, 1895), 217; from Chapter 31: "The Sexton's Old Horse."

7   *The Complete Poems of C. Day Lewis* (Stanford, CA: Stanford University Press, 1992), 546.

8   From the Paschal (or Catechetical) Homily ascribed to St John Chrysostom (PG 59:721–24), which is always read at the Paschal vigil in the Orthodox Church.

9   Clement of Alexandria, *Stromata* (*Stromateis*) 7.12 (ANF 2:543). Of course, this definition is hardly unique to Clement. Plato's Socrates defines it precisely this way: "Is it anything else than the separation of the soul from the body? Do we believe that death is this, namely, that the body comes to be separated by itself apart from the soul, and the soul comes to be separated by itself apart from the body? Is death anything else than that?" *Phaedo* 64c; *Complete Works*, 56.

10 St Maximus the Confessor, *Four Hundred Texts on Love* 2.93; English translation: *Philokalia* 2:81. St Gregory Palamas draws the two definitions together: "As the separation of the soul from the body is the death of the body, so the separation of God from the soul is the death of the soul. And this death of the soul is the true death. This is made clear by the commandment given in paradise, when God

said to Adam, 'On whatever day you eat from the forbidden tree you will certainly die' (cf. Gen. 2.17). And it was indeed Adam's soul that died by becoming through his transgression separated from God; for bodily he continued to live after that time, even for nine hundred and thirty years (cf. Gen. 5.5)." *To the Most Reverend Nun Xenia* 9; English translation: *Philokalia* 4:296.

11 Plato famously referred to the body as both tomb (*Gorgias* 493a) and prison (*Phaedo* 82e–83a, with intentional irony: Socrates says this in prison as he awaits execution).

12 C. G. Jung, *Modern Man in Search of a Soul* (London: Routledge-Ark Paperbacks, 1984), 253.

13 Dostoevsky, *Brothers Karamazov,* 50 (1.2.3: "Women of Faith").

14 Ultimately the image of the clay pot is scriptural (e.g. Jer 18.1–6; Is 64.8; Rom 9.21–23; 2 Cor 4.7; etc.), but it was used by several Church Fathers to describe the resurrection, beginning with St Methodius (*On the Resurrection* 1.44) and then further elaborated by others, like St Gregory of Nyssa (*Catechetical Discourse* 8.3): "For since by a movement of free will we gained fellowship with evil . . . and by this falling away from the blessedness of a dispassionate understanding we were transformed to vice, on account of this man is dissolved again 'into the earth' like some 'clay vessel,' so that, the filth now shut up within him being separated out, he might be re-formed by the resurrection to the

form [he had] from the beginning, if indeed he preserves
what is according to the image in the present life." St Gregory of Nyssa, *Catechetical Discourse: A Handbook for Cat-
echists*, trans. Ignatius Green, Popular Patristics Series 60
(Yonkers, NY: St Vladimir's Seminary Press, 2019), 83–84.

15 Evlogitaria for the Dead, from the Funeral Service (and the
memorial service, called in the Slav tradition the Panikhida);
English translation: *Panikhida and Funeral* (South Canaan,
PA: St Tikhon's Monastery Press, 2017), 11, 66.

16 *The Writings of Saint Francis of Assisi*, trans. Paschal Rob-
inson (Philadelphia: The Dolphin Press, 1906), 153.

17 Nicholas Arseniev, *Russian Piety* (London: Faith Press,
1964), 90.